MW00878901

THE IRONCLADS

Frank R. Donovan

MERICAN HERITAGE • NEW WORD CITY

INTRODUCTION

The famous battle between the *Monitor* and the *Merrimac* (CSS *Virginia*) at Hampton Roads, Virginia, on March 9, 1862, marked the end of one era in naval history and the beginning of another. It introduced the age of the ironclad, which was to rule the seas for some eighty years, but it was not so much the cause of the change as the announcement that the change had come. The *Monitor* and the *Merrimac* were not the world's first ironclads, but they put on the world's first fight between ironclads, proving something that many naval experts already suspected to be true - that the day of the wooden warship was ended forever.

This truth was emphasized again and again during the Civil War, much to the advantage of the North.

Largely because the North had the industrial capacity to build many more armored ships than the South, the Confederacy was never able to control some of its own most important rivers or quite break the North's blockade of its shores. Yet it did marvels with the inadequate industrial resources it had. Some of its creations - like the *Tennessee,* for instance, an ironclad ram that gave Admiral David Farragut and his partly wooden fleet a good deal of trouble at Mobile - were remarkable. But the South never was really able to compete in this field.

For at least a generation after the war, the world's navies experimented with ironclads. The experimentation was so vigorous and continuous that, for many years, warships were beginning to be obsolescent as soon as they were commissioned. There was a race between guns and armor, until it began at last to be seen - after the twentieth century was well along - that no amount of armor could make a ship invulnerable the way the *Merrimac* and *Monitor* had been. Perfection of the submarine, the airplane, and, above all, the torpedo finally sealed the case. In the 1940s, the battleship - the enormously enlarged descendant of the *Monitor* - became as out-of-date as the heavily armored dinosaur.

So the story of the ironclad is one locked in the past. But in it is a fascinating chapter that found its dramatic beginning at Hampton Roads when two clumsy, hastily improvised vessels showed the world just what might happen when one ironclad fought another.

1
"THAT THING
IS COMING DOWN
THE RIVER"

March 8, 1862, was a sunny, still Saturday at Hampton Roads. The long, shallow bay that carries the waters of the Elizabeth and James rivers into Chesapeake Bay was lined with the white tents and threatening cannons of the Confederacy on the south bank and of the Union on the north. Twelve thousand Union troops occupied Fort Monroe and the land immediately north of it. However, they represented only a tenuous foothold for the Union in otherwise solid Confederate territory. The fort stood guard at the entrance of the Roads.

Under Fort Monroe's guns lay three of the North's most powerful warships, the wooden steam frigates *Minnesota*, *St. Lawrence*, and *Roanoke*.

Almost ten miles away, two other Union ships, the sailing frigate *Congress* and the sloop of war *Cumberland*, guarded the river mouths. There were no Confederate ships in sight: The little Southern flotilla of two converted passenger vessels and three tiny gunboats sat helpless in the James River, bottled up by Northern ships and shore batteries.

The Northern vessels themselves had been on the alert for a month. Union intelligence sources had warned them that the Confederates were building an iron-armored warship at Norfolk, up the Elizabeth River. Each day had brought new rumors that this ironclad monster was going to attack. Yet, as day followed day and the Southern vessel still did not appear, the sailors of the Union Navy began to relax.

This crisp March morning, they grumbled and wondered why they could not have galley fires and hot food. On the deck of the USS *Congress*, an officer looked through his spyglass toward the Elizabeth River and suddenly stiffened. "I think that thing is coming down the river," he said to a fellow officer. Then a moment later, a signal gun cracked from a Union gunboat at the mouth of the Elizabeth, and every man strained to look. Far up the river, they made out a plume of smoke hanging over a low, slowly moving mass. The monster was coming out at last.

What was the monster? She was, at least in the vital parts of her hull, the gallant U.S. Navy ship *Merrimac* which had fallen into Southern hands when the war began. First built and launched in 1855, the *Merrimac* was one of six conventional wooden frigates that the tradition-bound Navy had ordered instead of the experimental ironclad warships that were just beginning to be built in Europe. This was the second Navy ship to be named for Massachusetts's Merrimack River, which flows through the town of Merrimac - leading to some confusion over the spelling. (The first USS *Merrimack*, commissioned in 1798, saw action in the Quasi-War between the United States and France before being sold as a merchant ship and renamed the *Monticello*.) The five other frigates in her class – the first in the United States to be driven by propeller - were also named for rivers: the *Wabash, Roanoke, Niagara, Minnesota,* and *Colorado.*

The *Merrimac* was a tall, graceful beauty whose towering clouds of snowy canvas almost hid the ugly smokestack that rose from her cranky steam engines below deck. As flagship of the Pacific fleet, the *Merrimac* had sailed to ports in England and France and proudly carried the Stars and Stripes around Cape Horn, cruising the coast of South and Central America. In November 1859, the ship headed home, docking early the next year at the navy yard on the Elizabeth River near Norfolk, Virginia, for much-needed engine repairs.

Officially decommissioned from the U.S. Navy on February 16, 1860, the *Merrimac* was stripped of its armaments – fourteen eight-inch guns, two ten-inch guns, and twenty-four nine-inch smoothbore mounted cannons that had been designed by U.S. Navy Rear Admiral John A. Dahlgren in 1849. The ship's service to her nation was considered complete. The election of President Abraham Lincoln on November 6, 1860, changed everything.

The leaders of Southern slave-holding states, convinced Lincoln's policies were a threat to their way of life, had pledged secession if the Republican were elected. Little more than a month later, on December 20, South Carolina was the first to keep this promise. Before Lincoln could be sworn in as president on March 4, six other states – Mississippi, Florida, Alabama, Georgia, Louisiana, and Texas – had followed suit, forming the Confederate States of America and electing as its president Jefferson Davis, a former U.S. Army officer. This new sovereign nation, not satisfied with merely disavowing itself of the Union's laws, seemed to be girding for war.

President Lincoln saw the dissolution of the Union as intolerable, but first tried to reason with the South. "We are not enemies, but friends. . . . We must not be enemies," he said in his inaugural address. "The mystic chords of memory, stretching from every battlefield, and patriot grave, to every living heart and hearthstone, all over this broad land, will yet swell the chorus of the Union, when again touched, as surely they will be, by the better angels of our nature." States in the upper South had so far rejected secession; none were more divided than Virginia, where the issue would give birth to a new state, West Virginia, in May 1861.

Virginia delegates had called a convention on February 13, 1861, to consider joining the Confederacy. The motion was defeated on April 4, but reconsidered and passed eleven days later. Between those two votes, the Civil War had begun. The first shots had been fired in the Battle of Fort Sumter in South Carolina. Fort Sumter dominated Charleston harbor and was the last Union stronghold in the state, which after its secession had ordered all federal property turned over. Ignoring a Confederate ultimatum to evacuate the fort, Lincoln instead sent ships to resupply U.S. Army Major Robert Anderson's troops there. On April 12, the Confederate Army laid siege on the fort, which was surrendered without casualties on either side two days later. Lincoln responded by calling on every state in the Union to send 75,000 troops to recapture forts, protect Washington, and preserve the Union. Rather than comply, Virginia seceded, and its state capital, Richmond, became the heart of the Confederacy.

Union Assets

The *Merrimac* was still at Norfolk when Virginia demanded the surrender of the navy shipyard. Anticipating a run on federal assets in the South, U.S. Secretary of the Navy Gideon Welles had taken steps to protect the Norfolk shipyard. One of the navy's largest and most productive shipyards, Norfolk also had one of only two dry docks in the country, making it a priority for Welles. But Lincoln, still careful to avoid inciting war in March 1861, had ordered Welles not to make any personnel changes or otherwise take action that could be construed as hostile or defensive. With the precision of a surgeon, Welles dispatched the steamship USS *Pocahontas* to the shipyard on March 14, under the guise of repairing storm damage. The ship's true purpose was defense of the shipyard, though Welles believed it would not be enough.

On March 23, the fifty-gun frigate USS *Cumberland,* the flagship of the Home Squadron during the Mexican-American War, arrived at the Norfolk navy yard for repairs. The *Cumberland* crew was ordered to monitor the situation, and back up the *Pocahontas* if needed in battle. Welles's persistent requests for troops to guard the yard, however, were denied, and the navy secretary began to abandon any hope of holding it. His new priority was to keep the ships docked there, and their weaponry, from falling into Confederate hands.

The Norfolk shipyard held mostly relics, but also some valuable, seaworthy vessels. Besides the *Pocahontas* and the *Cumberland*, these included the sloop-of-war *Plymouth* and forty-year-old *Delaware*. The *Merrimac* was worth as much as all the others combined. At 275 feet long, weighing 3,200 tons, she was one of the most powerful warships in the U.S. Navy, and Gideon Welles was determined that the *Merrimac* would continue to serve the Union. The secretary of the Navy prepared to move the ships from Norfolk, but was discouraged by reports that the *Merrimac* would not be ready to sail for at least a month.

In charge of the Norfolk yard, Commodore Charles Stewart MacCauley was sixty-eight years old and an alcoholic. Welles later described him as "faithful but feeble and incompetent for the crisis." The commandant, though, was not helped by his subordinate officers, several of whom were Southern sympathizers who had planned to preserve the yard and its ships for the Confederates. On April 10, Welles ordered MacCauley to work quickly to prepare the *Merrimac* to sail "to Philadelphia or to any other yard, should it be deemed necessary, or, in case of danger from unlawful attempts to take possession of her, that she may be placed beyond their reach." The next day, already doubting MacCauley's abilities, Welles dispatched Commander James Alden, aboard the steamship USS *South Carolina*, to push his agenda.

The siege of Fort Sumter on April 12 added even more urgency to the mission, and on the same day, Welles sent the U.S. Navy's top engineer, Benjamin Franklin Isherwood, to Norfolk. Isherwood told Welles that he thought he could have the *Merrimac* ready to sail in a week. But when he arrived at the shipyard on April 14, Isherwood discovered that the ship's engine had been almost completely disassembled. The engineer, authorized by Welles to take any action necessary to expedite the repairs, ordered the workmen to drop everything else. The crew was divided into two shifts, working around the clock. Still, time was running out.

On April 16, Welles ordered yet another commander to Norfolk. Hiram Paulding was a gruff, sixty-three-year-old rear admiral who had served the U.S. Navy since the War of 1812. But his presence at the shipyard only confused the situation. Paulding carried a letter from Welles to MacCauley stating that it "may not be necessary" for the *Merrimac* to sail to Philadelphia "unless there is immediate danger pending."

A rain storm that night provided cover for Confederates to sail into Chesapeake Bay, enter the natural harbor at Hampton Roads, and sink two eight-ton lightboats at the mouth of the Elizabeth River. The goal was to block the channel, to prevent evacuation of the ships at Norfolk. But the crew of the *Cumberland,* discovering the obstructions in the light of day, determined that they were sixteen feet deep – enough for even the massive *Merrimac* to pass over. Still, the proof of a Confederate plot raised anxiety at the shipyard; patrols were stepped up as engineers hurried repairs.

The work to get the *Merrimac* seaworthy again – which commanders had estimated would take a week to a month – was completed in seventy-two hours. Paulding watched as the ship was loaded with the coal that would carry her downriver and out of the bay to the Atlantic Ocean. Once fueled, all that remained was to replace the guns. Sensing the evacuation was in order, Paulding returned to Washington with a favorable report for Gideon Welles. But by the time he delivered this news, the situation was almost completely out of hand. Virginia delegates had voted, in secret session, to secede from the Union. And at the Norfolk shipyard, Commodore MacCauley was waffling.

Commander Alden and engineer Isherwood pressed MacCauley to give the evacuation order. Twice on April 18, the engines of the *Merrimac* were fired up and then doused. MacCauley, indecisive and drinking, was swayed by the secret secessionists among his subordinates, including ordnance officer John Tucker and executive officer Robert Robb (both of whom would go on to serve the Confederate States Navy with distinction).

They argued variously that the decision could wait, that the *Merrimac* was needed to defend the shipyard, and that the obstructions in the river would prevent the evacuation anyway. Tucker blocked the rearmament of the *Merrimac*, and Robb convinced MacCauley to rescind his order to turn the ship over to Alden. Arguments by Alden and Isherwood only temporarily penetrated the din. Frustrated, first Isherwood and then Alden returned to Washington to advise Welles, who was stunned by the turn of events.

The secretary of the navy placed much of the blame on Alden for failing to take charge. "Alden was timid but patriotic when there was no danger," Welles wrote later, "for he was endowed with great moral or physical courage, though he believed himself possessed of both, and was no doubt really anxious to do something without encountering enemies or taking upon himself much responsibility. At Norfolk, all his heroic drawing room resolution and good intentions failed him. A man of energy and greater will and force, with the orders of the Secretary, would have inspired and influenced MacCauley, whose heart was right, and carried out these orders."

Now, Welles believed he had no other option but to fight for the Norfolk shipyard. He easily convinced President Lincoln and his Cabinet of this. But stubborn "Old Fuss and Feathers" General-in-Chief Winfield

Scott still resisted sending troops to Virginia, now considered enemy territory. Finally, after much discussion, Scott relented, and Welles frantically called up reinforcements from shipyards in New York and Philadelphia.

Hiram Paulding set off again for Norfolk - this time with orders that left no doubt he was in charge. Welles realized, however, that the troops might arrive too late to save the shipyard, and planned a contingency. He instructed Paulding: "With the means placed at your command, you will do all in your power to protect and place beyond danger the vessels and property belonging to the United States. On no account should the arms and munitions be permitted to fall into the hands of insurrectionists, or those who would wrest them from the custody of the Government; and should it finally become necessary, you will, in order to prevent that result, destroy the property." At the Washington Naval Yard, the man-of-war ship *Pawnee* was stocked with the tools of that destruction: forty barrels of gunpowder, eleven tanks of turpentine, six brushes, twelve barrels of cotton waste, and 181 paper fuses.

The *Pawnee* sailed out of Washington late on April 19 with Paulding at the helm. Also on board were Commander James Alden, who no doubt hoped for some redemption, and captains Charles Wilkes and Horatio Wright, assigned to take command of ships harbored at Norfolk. The next afternoon, the

Pawnee arrived at Fort Monroe, on the southern tip of the Virginia Peninsula in Chesapeake Bay, where 360 volunteers of the Third Massachusetts Regiment boarded. It was 6:00 p.m. before the warship was on its way to Norfolk. Two hours before, Commodore MacCauley had given up hope of defending the yard and ordered the ships sunk. By the time Paulding arrived around 8:00, it was already too late.

MacCauley had reason to panic. His men had successfully thwarted, without bloodshed, a Confederate attempt to seize a Navy tugboat the day before. But, as word of Virginia's secession spread, nearly all of his officers had resigned their commissions to join the Confederacy, and his 800 workmen also abandoned the shipyard. Then, a Virginia militia had easily made off with 2,800 barrels of gunpowder from the magazine at old Fort Norfolk. Rumors swirled that an attack on the shipyard was imminent. "I understood that Virginia State troops were arriving at Portsmouth and Norfolk in numbers from Richmond, Petersburg, and the neighborhood," MacCauley reported, "and not having the means at my disposal to get the *Merrimac, Germantown* and *Plymouth* to a place of safety I determined on destroying them, being satisfied that with the small force under my command the yard was no longer tenable."

Only the *Cumberland* was spared from being scuttled. MacCauley had decided that this ship, with her captain and crew of 350 men, would hold off the Confederate attack for as long as a day, and then provide him with a means of retreat. The *Merrimac* engines were broken up as much as possible, her great shears hacked down, and the seacocks opened so that she started to fill with water. Relieving MacCauley of duty, Commodore Paulding hoped that some of the ships might still be salvageable. But the *Merrimac*, though not yet fully submerged, was flooded past its orlop deck and boilers. To raise her would take time that the U.S. Navy no longer had.

Paulding divided up the work of destroying the shipyard: a team to burn the scuttled ships, another to burn the buildings, and a third to blow up the dry dock. A hundred men with sledgehammers failed to break up the guns that had been stripped from the ships. MacCauley, drunk and despondent, had to be coaxed from his office onto the *Pawnee*. Trails of gunpowder, connecting to the turpentine-soaked ships and buildings, were designed to give the Navy men time to get safely away. At 4:20 a.m. on April 21, a signal flare was fired from the deck of the *Pawnee,* and the Norfolk shipyard burst into flame.

From the Ashes

Within hours, the Virginia militia entered the yard to extinguish it, and salvage what it could – which turned out to be a lot. General William B. Taliaferro, who commanded the militia, reported that "the damage was not so great as that at first apprehended. Only an inconsiderable portion of the property, with the exception of the ships, was destroyed, and some of the ships may yet be made serviceable." Somehow, the dry dock was left intact, the gunpowder fuse having failed to ignite. As the fires died, the Confederates realized they had been left with a tremendous arsenal: More than 1,000 guns that were easily reparable, 2,000 barrels of gunpowder, and even more ammunition. But the biggest prize lay just below the surface of the Elizabeth River.

The upper deck of the *Merrimac* was scorched, but parts that were submerged – the hull, engines, and boiler - had been protected from the fire. The first and foremost job of the Confederates who took over the shipyard was to raise the ship and tow it into the dry dock. A local salvage company was hired, for $6,000, to oversee the weeks-long project. The Confederate Navy's chief engineer, William P. Williamson, examined the *Merrimac,* and suggested that the engine could be fixed. The secretary of the Confederate Navy, Stephen Russell Mallory, a former U.S. Senator from Florida, soon gave more specific orders regarding the *Merrimac.*

Appointed by Confederate President Jefferson Davis in February 1861, Mallory was in charge of a

Navy with very few ships. Two months later, he had gained, with the Union's abandonment of Norfolk, the resources of the country's most extensive naval yard. Now he looked to buy and build a fleet that could stand up to the North. His first move was to seek out merchant vessels in Southern ports and Canada that could be converted to warships. When that effort came up short, he defied conventional wisdom and set his sights higher.

Mallory recognized that the naval success of the Confederacy depended on "fighting with iron against wood." From his experience in the Senate, he knew that the U.S. Navy had been slow to embrace the new iron-faced ships that were being rolled out in Europe and was determined to take advantage of that weakness. "I regard the possession of an iron-armored ship as a matter of the first necessity," Mallory wrote to the Committee on Naval Affairs. "Such a vessel at this time could traverse the entire coast of the United States, prevent all blockades, and encounter, with a fair prospect of success, their entire Navy."

France had been first to this well of innovation, launching in 1859 its *La Gloire* ("Glory"), a 5,630-ton broadside ship whose wooden hull was covered in armored plates twelve centimeters thick. A year later, England had debuted the iron-hulled HMS *Warrior*, weighing a massive 9,137 tons. Mallory had the French model in mind when he sent two agents, with $2 million, to London to arrange for the purchase or construction of two such ships for the Confederate Navy. But the European nations had declared neutrality in the Americans' war, and the shipbuilders there hesitated to fill Mallory's order. A London company did agree to build six, propeller-driven steamships – whose purpose, it could argue, had been misconstrued as commercial - for the Confederates.

A special committee of three naval experts advised Mallory that the quickest and least expensive way to get an ironclad - as these armored ships were beginning to be called - was to build an iron casemate, or fortified gun enclosure, on top of the *Merrimac's* wooden hull. She had already been stripped to her lowest deck, and it would be a relatively easy job to convert the once-beautiful sailing swan into an ugly, but deadly, iron duckling.

The first designs were sketched by thirty-four-year-old Lieutenant John Mercer Brooke. A marine and military genius, Brooke had joined the U.S. Navy at fourteen and graduated from the naval academy at twenty-two. Working with the U.S. Naval Observatory, he had developed a device for measuring the depth of the Pacific Ocean. He would also give the Confederate States Navy the Brooke Rifle – a muzzle-loading naval and coastal defense gun that fired both armor-piercing and explosive shells, which he also designed. He envisioned the Confederate ship with armored eaves that extended two feet below the waterline, and a false bow and stern above – super-structures made of ship iron and decked over.

Secretary Mallory next recruited a naval constructor – or architect – named John Luke Porter for the project. A native of Virginia, forty-eight-year-old Porter had been stationed at the Norfolk shipyard when it was abandoned; his first assignment in the Confederate States Navy was to help assess the value of what had been left behind by the Union. Ironclads had interested him for some time, so when he arrived in Mallory's Richmond office, he presented a model that he had designed – almost identical to Brooke's sketches. It was agreed that the fineries of Brooke's version – the shape and extension of the hull – would add speed and buoyancy to the craft. For the rest of their lives, Porter and Brooke would each claim to have designed the ironclad that the Confederate States Navy would commission the CSS *Virginia*.

Work on the *Merrimac* began in July 1861. Porter, the architect, was in charge of the overall conversion of the ship; Brooke, the gunman, took responsibility for manufacturing the iron plate and heavy ordnance. Chief engineer William Williamson, meanwhile, oversaw repairs and modifications to the ship's machinery. The first job was to cut the burned timbers of the hull down past the original waterline, with just enough clearance for the ship's large, twin-bladed screw propeller.

Although 1,500 men labored on the vessel, progress was slow. Most of those laborers had never worked on a ship before. Nor did they have the right tools. Except for wood, all other materials - like nuts and bolts - were in short supply, for the Confederacy lacked heavy industry. In fact, the biggest bottleneck in building a Southern ironclad was iron.

Early specifications for the *Merrimac* called for approximately 1,000 tons of iron plate to armor her. However, at the beginning of the Civil War, there were few iron manufacturers anywhere in the South and only one near enough Norfolk to supply the navy yard. Though an ironclad ship of war was desperately needed to help the Confederate Navy keep seaports open to foreign trade, iron in the form of railroads and artillery equipment was equally necessary for the Army. So the *Merrimac* was allotted only a small share of the limited supply of iron - just part of what she required. Much of the iron that went into the *Merrimac* came from the Norfolk shipyard – 300 tons from old tools, obsolete cannons, and ship fittings destroyed in the fire – and rail torn up in the Shenandoah Valley to disrupt Union communications. But Brooke soon doubled, then quadrupled the iron order after tests proved the original one-inch plates would not hold up to his big guns. He now called for two layers of two-inch iron to encase the *Merrimac*'s wooden hull. Operations at the Tredegar Iron Works in Richmond now became devoted exclusively to rolling out two-inch iron plates for the *Merrimac*, at a negotiated price of six and a half cents per pound.

While they worked with wood and waited for iron, Williamson labored over the engines. They had never been very good engines; they had needed repair when the frigate put in at Norfolk, and lying on the river bottom had not improved them. But they were the only marine engines the South had available, and Williamson had to make them work.

After dismissing an engineer for insubordination early on, Williamson was gifted with a uniquely qualified assistant. Twenty-five-year-old H. Ashton Ramsay had served aboard the *Merrimac* during its Pacific tour and was intimate with the engine failings. "From my past and present experience with the engines of this vessel, I am of the opinion that they cannot be relied upon," Ramsay reported. "During a cruise of two years . . . they were continually breaking down, at times when least expected." Larger than most at the time, the ship's engines had been built by the West Point Foundry in Cold Spring, New York, using deficient material – shortcomings that Ramsay "set to work to correct as far as possible, with the limited means at my command."

Porter carefully directed engineering of the ship's delicate inner fittings, from hawse pipes to steering gear. Brooke called for modifications – the addition of four gun ports and doubling the hatches from two to four – that caused delays when implemented. Along with Williamson, their attentions also were diverted to other duties associated with their positions in the Confederate Navy. They were busy, and exhausted, though engineer Ramsay believed more could, and should, be done. The shipyard, he complained, "should be full of mechanics," working without rest to complete the crucial instrument of war.

For a while, the yard was filled, not with workmen, but spectators - "crowds of people, idle soldiers and others," Ramsay said later, who "used to assemble around the dry dock, and express their opinions . . . ." The prevailing opinion of these onlookers was that the iron beast "would go to the bottom as soon as she sank below the knuckle . . ." said Ramsay. An old friend of the engineer's, Captain Charles McIntosh, said before leaving for a command at New Orleans: "Good-bye, Ramsay, I shall never see you again; she will be your coffin." But interspersed among the critics were spies, who carried reports of the ironclad's progress to the Union, and soon security was heightened. Flag Officer French Forrest, commandant of the yard, ordered that no one could enter the shipyard without a written pass from an officer. He also required the workmen to swear an oath of loyalty to the Confederacy. Still, information leaked North.

Launching the *Virginia*

Almost a year's frantic work went into converting the USS *Merrimac* into the ironclad CSS *Virginia*. Finally commissioned in February 1862, the ship was ordered into action the morning of March 8 by Captain Franklin Buchanan. Even then, she was not quite finished. The steel shutters that were to shield her gun ports were still lying on the dock, and so were the solid steel projectiles for her guns. But Buchanan, a former superintendent of the U.S. Naval Academy, thought these would not be needed. He took comfort from the fact that the explosive shells he did have aboard were more effective against wooden vessels - and every Union ship in Hampton Roads was made of wood.

Carpenters and mechanics were still at work on the *Virginia, too*. As the officers issued crisp orders, the workmen scurried ashore with their tools. Then some 300 men of the *Virginia*'s new crew boarded the ship, most of them uncertain about what to do or where to go.

There had been some clamoring by officers for command positions about the ship, despite the public's lack of faith in its seaworthiness. French Forrest and others had vied to captain the ship, but Buchanan - in charge of assigning officers as head of the Office of Orders and Detail – reserved that post for himself. Ramsay went aboard as the ship's chief engineer. John Mercer Brooke, hoping to inspire confidence in the vessel he designed, fought Secretary of the Navy Stephen Mallory for a spot on the *Virginia*, but ultimately was kept ashore by a family illness.

Mounting a crew proved more difficult. There were few sailors in the Southern farming states. And at the onset of war, most of those sailors had joined the Confederate Army, which was reluctant to give them up to the Navy. Still, many were enticed to switch. Any man who was discharged from the Army and enlisted in the Navy for three years was paid $20 in January 1862; the next month, that bounty was increased to $50. As a result, most of the *Virginia*'s crew were soldiers recently reassigned from artillery regiments. Many of them had never been on a ship before.

The *Virginia*'s ten guns had not been fired since they were put aboard, and her engines had never moved the great bulk from the dock, but now black smoke belched from her stack. She began to move, and suddenly it looked as though she might be capable of doing the job for which she had been designed. Mallory seemed to have no qualms about the *Virginia*'s abilities. His orders to Captain Buchanan were less instructive than a testament of expectations:

> The *Virginia* is a novelty in naval construction, is untried, and her powers unknown, and the Department will not

give specific orders as to her attack upon the enemy. Her powers as a ram are regarded as very formidable, and it is hoped that you may be able to test them.

Like the bayonet charge of the infantry, this mode of attack, while the most distinctive, will commend itself to you in the present scarcity of ammunition. It is one also that may be rendered destructive at night against the enemy at anchor.

Even without guns the ship would be formidable as a ram.

Could you pass Old Point and make a dashing cruise on the Potomac as far as Washington, its effect upon the public mind would be important to the cause.

The condition of our country . . . demand our utmost exertions, and convinced as I am that the opportunity and the means of striking a decided blow for our Navy are now for the first time presented, I congratulate you upon it, and know that your judgment and gallantry will meet all just expectations.

Action – prompt and successful action – now would be of serious importance to our cause.

Buchanan intended to waste no time in putting the *Virginia* to the test Mallory had spelled out. By some accounts, collision bulkheads had been added at the bow and stern only after it became clear that the North was making progress on its own ironclad to rival the *Virginia*. But John Brooke later claimed that "we always intended that she should be a ram. All ironclad vessels are built as rams." Preparing for the ship's trial run, Buchanan summoned his chief engineer from the engine room. He posed a question probably considered odd by crew members, so far uninformed of the captain's true intentions: "Ramsay, what would happen to your engines if there should be a collision?"

Fifteen miles away, at the natural harbor of Hampton Roads, where the Elizabeth and James rivers meet before entering the Chesapeake Bay, a fleet of Union ships had set up a blockade. The USS *Cumberland*, which had been part of the operation that left the former *Merrimac* to burn, had returned. She had been repaired in Boston, after damages to her hull while being towed by the *Pawnee* over obstructions meant to prevent their escape from Norfolk the year before. The *Cumberland* had also been upgraded to a new seventy-pounder rifle, which the ship's gunmen had so far had no use for. All had been quiet at Hampton Roads. On the morning of March 8, the crews of the *Cumberland* and the nearby USS *Congress* were leisurely washing their clothes and running them up the rigging to dry – unaware that a battle was brewing.

"I am going to ram the *Cumberland*," Captain Buchanan at last announced to his officers on the *Virginia*. "I'm told she has the new rifle guns, the only ones in their whole fleet we have cause to fear. The moment we are in the Roads I'm going to make right for her and ram her." Most of the crew, though, continued to work under the assumption that this was a drill.

Word quickly spread through the towns of Norfolk and Portsmouth, on the other side of the Elizabeth River, that the *Virginia* was on the move. Crowds gathered along the riverbank to see the odd behemoth, which above water resembled a pitched barn roof with a tall smokestack. Today, it might be mistaken for a primitive submarine. From her stern flew the "Stars and Bars" of the Confederate national flag. Some spectators stood on rooftops, waving hats and handkerchiefs as the ironclad passed. At Craney Island, a Confederate fort in Portsmouth, troops cheered wildly, and the river had filled with all sorts of vessels – from Army tugs to oyster skiffs – angling for a view of the action.

2

"I'LL GO DOWN WITH MY COLORS FLYING"

On the *Virginia* came, an ungainly but deadly monster. The Northerners knew that this was the moment they had been waiting for. Boatswain's pipes shrilled on the guard ships. Wash lines came down, and topsails were loosed. Signal flags were run up the rigging. Far down Hampton Roads, the frigates prepared for action. Without waiting to get up steam, they passed lines to scurrying tugs to tow them into battle. In single file, the big ships moved up the Roads, exchanging fire with the Confederate shore guns as they passed. The range was too great for much harm to be done, but the clouds of white smoke, the tall ships heeling from the recoil of the broadsides, and the sparkling light reflected off shells splashing into the water gave a vivid impression of battle.

A mile and a half from the upper end of the Roads, misfortune already began to plague the Northern fleet. The *Minnesota* ran aground; behind her, the *Roanoke* stuck in the mud; at the end of the line, the crew of the *St. Lawrence found themselves* grounded. These big steam frigates, mounting a total of 130 guns, would be no help to their sailing sisters.

Meanwhile, the slow-moving *Virginia* reached the mouth of the river. Even running with the current, the engines could not move the vast bulk of the ironclad at much more than five miles an hour. A whisper was heard among the ironclad crew: "If this is all the speed we can make, we better get out and walk." It was shortly after 1:00 p.m., and the men aboard the Union vessels could see her plainly now. The sun glistened on the pork fat with which her sides had been greased to make boarding harder and to help deflect cannon balls.

The 320 men of the *Virginia* had crowded on the topside deck to hear their captain's call to arms, which engineer Ramsay later recounted: "Sailors, in a few moments, you will have the long expected opportunity to show your devotion to our cause. Remember that you are about to strike for your country, for your homes, for your wives and your children." They rushed then to their stations.

Not alone, the *Virginia* was the flagship of the James River squadron, and two of her sister ships – the *Raleigh* and the *Beaufort* – escorted her toward the

James River, where the other three waited for an opening to engage. The first shot of the Battle of Hampton Roads was fired by the *Beaufort*, but fell short; Captain William Harwar Parker, who gave the order, was later reprimanded by Buchanan for it. A preliminary skirmish between the *Beaufort* and the Union tugboat *Zouave* had no effect. Buchanan held his fire until he was less than a mile away from the Union fleet.

The frigate *Congress* was the nearest Union ship, and with fifty guns, she was the strongest. She stood ready to receive the monster's attack, but Captain Buchanan changed the *Virginia's* course and steered away toward the sloop *Cumberland*. Churning the water, she moved even more slowly now than she had on her way downriver. The heavy ironclad drew twenty-two feet of water, but Hampton Roads was only that deep in the center of the channel. Her keel and rudder were dragging through mud.

As the *Virginia* headed toward the *Cumberland*, she passed within range of the *Congress* and the two ships exchanged broadsides. The shells of the Union frigate bounced off the grease-smeared sides of the ironclad to burst harmlessly in the air or to fall hissing into the water. The crew of the *Virginia* gave a mighty cheer, for their monster had passed its first test.

The tide had swung the *Cumberland* so that her bow was facing the oncoming *Virginia*; in this position, only two of her guns could be brought to bear on the ironclad. With sails useless in the still air, the sloop's commander had to find other means of swinging her into position so that the broadside guns could be brought into action. He ordered a line run from the stern to the anchor cable to pull her around, but the tide was too strong.

When the *Virginia* came within range of the *Cumberland*, her bow gun spoke. The shell burst against the rail of the sloop and mowed down nine men. A second shell hit one of the bow guns, putting it out of action and killing or wounding all but one of the sixteen-man gun crew. The *Cumberland* opened fire with her remaining bow gun, one of the heavy cannons that Buchanan had feared. He need not have worried. The ten-inch shell bounced harmlessly off the *Virginia*'s bow.

As the ironclad crept toward the sloop, the single-gun duel continued, for the *Virginia* was not in a position to use her broadside guns either. When thirty men on the *Cumberland* tried to move up a gun to replace the one that had been disabled, a Confederate shell burst amidst the group, killing most of them. But Buchanan did not intend to sink the *Cumberland* with his guns. Below the water line, his ship carried another deadly weapon - the 1,500-pound, plow-shaped iron ram which jutted menacingly from her bow.

The *Virginia* turned as she came alongside the *Cumberland* and drove directly toward the vessel's side. The great weight of the ironclad pushed the ram through the wooden hull like a giant spear. As water rushed into the sloop, the *Cumberland* heeled over and seemed about to fall on her attacker. On the *Virginia's* gun deck, Executive Officer Catesby Jones noted: "The shock to us on striking was slight." But the impact caused a tremor to run through the engine room; chief engineer Ramsay recalled "an ominous pause, then a crash, shaking us all off our feet."

Aboard the *Cumberland,* a young doctor described what happened next: "The *[Virginia]* tries to back out; the tide is making . . . it slews her around; the weakened ram breaks off; she leaves it in the *Cumberland.* The battle rages. Broadside answers broadside and the sanded deck is red and slippery with the blood of the wounded and the dying; they are dragged amidships. There is no one and no time to take them below. Delirium seizes the crew; they strip to their trousers; tie handkerchiefs around their heads; kick off their shoes; fight and yell like demons; load and fire at will."

With water pouring in through the jagged hole in her side, the *Cumberland* was doomed. Captain Buchanan poked his head out a hatch and shouted to her commander, Lieutenant George Morris, "Do you surrender?" Morris yelled back, "Never! I'll go down with my colors flying." With the four guns of its broadside, the ironclad continued to blast the sinking ship. The shells exploded against the *Cumberland's* wooden sides, sending splinters and pieces of steel flying across the gun deck. Soon, more than half of the 190 men at the guns were stretched on the deck, wounded or dead. The survivors continued to fire harmless shells against the iron sides of the Southern ship. Not a man left his post. No ship in the United States Navy ever fought more bravely than the *Cumberland*.

As water rose around the feet of the men on the gun deck, Morris shouted, "Save all who can!" Some men dived through the open gun ports toward shore. Others ran up to the spar deck to help man the guns that could still be worked on this level. The ship lurched, and the forward gun fired a final shot as the bow sank beneath the surface. An aftergun broke loose and hurtled down the steeply slanted deck, crushing a man who was about to leap for safety. The *Cumberland* went to the bottom, carrying the ram of the *Virginia*, many dead and wounded, and the ship's chaplain, Methodist minister John L. Lenhart, who stayed to pray with the injured. Lenhart was the first Navy chaplain to die in battle. The water was so shallow that the masts stuck out above the surface, one of them still flying the Stars and Stripes.

When Lieutenant Joseph B. Smith, commander of the *Congress*, saw the effect of the *Virginia* ram on the *Cumberland*, he tried to save his ship from the same fate by having her towed into shallow water where the ironclad could not reach her. He did not know that the deadly ram was now lying at the bottom of the Roads. A little steam tug, the *Zouave*, pulled the wooden vessel under the protection of the Union shore batteries. There the *Congress* grounded with her stern toward the channel and only the two after-guns usable.

Lieutenant Smith was happily surprised when the *Virginia* steamed past him and on up the James River. But his relief was short-lived. Buchanan had only gone up to a wider part of the channel to turn around. Going up and coming back, the ironclad was raked without effect by the Union batteries on the riverbank. Buchanan's return fire smashed some of the gun emplacements and drove the men to cover. A small boat put out from the ironclad, and its crew coolly captured a Union sloop that was anchored under the shore guns. After the ironclad passed, the shore batteries opened fire on the vessels of the little Confederate James River squadron. During the battle, they had seen a long-awaited chance to move out of the river, and had made a reckless but successful dash into Hampton Roads to join their big sister, the *Virginia*.

On returning downriver, the *Virginia* took position about 200 yards astern of the *Congress* and started to rake her with broadsides. Smith doubled the crews on his after-guns to increase fire power and formed a chain of men to pass powder along the deck. A shell from the *Virginia* cut down the line of sailors, exploding the powder in their hands. A second shell dismantled one stern gun; a third hit the other gun squarely on the muzzle; a fourth killed Lieutenant Smith. Lieutenant Garrett J. Pendergrast took over the command.

The young officer faced a difficult decision. Although surrender was disgraceful, his ship was afire below decks, and 120 of her men were already dead. Blood was running down the side of the hull and dripping on the deck of the tug *Zouave*, which was standing by. He could not bring another gun to bear on the ironclad. He could not even go down with his ship - she was already on the bottom. Unable either to defend or save the vessel, he surrendered.

Buchanan sent two of the James River gunboats to accept the surrender, help take the wounded off, and destroy the ship. The Union land forces fired on the gunboats, and in the process killed some of their own men on the *Congress*. The Union commander on shore had not been able to follow clearly the swift-moving events in the Roads because of the heavy gun smoke surrounding the ships, and he probably had not seen the white surrender flag go up.

Buchanan, who had come up on deck to direct the evacuation of his Union prisoners, was seriously wounded in the hail of cannon and rifle fire from the shore. Enraged at what he considered a violation of the surrender, he ordered his men to "Plug hot shot into her and don't leave her until she's afire. They must look after their own wounded since they won't let us." It was a painful order for Buchanan to give. His brother was paymaster of the *Congress* and was perhaps one of those wounded. The few cannon balls that the *Virginia* carried as incendiary shot were rolled into a furnace and, when red hot, were hurled through the wooden sides of the *Congress*. She began to blaze furiously.

With Buchanan wounded, the *Virginia*'s executive officer, Lieutenant Catesby Jones, took command and looked around for the next victim. The grounded *Minnesota* was nearest, a mile and a half away. The *Roanoke* had gotten off the shoals and retreated to Fort Monroe. The *St. Lawrence* was still aground far down the Roads. Jones told the civilian pilots of the *Virginia* to bring her closer to the *Minnesota*. They replied that the water was too shallow. For an hour, the two ships fought a long-range duel, their shells skipping over the surface of the calm water, doing little or no damage.

Meanwhile, the *Virginia* had begun to leak at the bow where the ram had broken off, and there were so many shell holes in her stack that there was not enough draft for the boiler fires. The men were exhausted from four hours of fighting. As night approached, the pilots told Jones that the tide was ebbing, and if he did not leave promptly, his ship would have to spend the night in the Roads. Then, if a wind came up, waves might sweep into the low, open gun ports and swamp her. At 5:00 p.m., Jones reluctantly gave the order to take the ironclad back to the deeper water of the Elizabeth River and anchor for the night. The *Minnesota* would still be there in the morning. After sinking her, the monster could finish off the rest of the wooden ships in the Roads, run past Fort Monroe, and start a career of widespread destruction and blockade-breaking that might help the South toward victory in the Civil War. Or so Jones thought.

But tomorrow would be a different day. No one at Hampton Roads knew that at the very moment when the South's secret weapon was creating havoc in the bay, the North's counter weapon was slowly approaching. While the *Virginia*'s shells were pouring into the stricken *Congress*, a strange looking little ship named the *Monitor* was rounding Cape Henry, ready to do battle.

3
"IT STRIKES ME THERE'S SOMETHING IN IT"

Union Naval Secretary Gideon Welles had very little time to think about ironclads in the war's early days. President Abraham Lincoln had given him a more pressing problem. The president had ordered a naval blockade of the 3,000-mile-long Confederate coastline. The Union had only forty-two vessels available to carry out this order. What it needed most urgently was not one or two powerful ships, but hundreds, whatever their size and armament.

So the Union began to build an unparalleled number of ships, to buy and rent freighters, tugs, passenger liners, river boats, pilot boats, and even ferryboats if they could mount a gun. Within four months of the siege on Fort Sumter, the

United States Navy had forty-seven ships under construction. Before the war ended, the North had 600 vessels on blockade duty. Only after that armada had begun to be gathered would the Navy Department consider the novel idea of building ships with iron sides.

The idea was not only novel but unthinkable and unacceptable to conservative naval designers. They continued to regard tough oak as the only proper material for a big warship - just as it had been considered for hundreds of years. Their opinion did not change when a few European ships were constructed with iron sides, nor even when steam engines became powerful and dependable enough to move the far heavier vessels at a reasonable speed. However, in 1824, a French colonel named Henri Paixhans invented a gun that could safely throw an explosive shell as straight and as far as a cannon ball. Such shells could penetrate and set fire to the toughest oak. Their increasing use sounded the death knell for wooden ships. But few people realized that the era of the lofty beauties had ended until the war between Russia and Turkey in the 1850s.

Emperor Napoleon III of France, an ally of the Turks, was the first national leader to acknowledge that unarmored wooden ships could not stand up to explosive shells. When the war erupted, he promptly ordered the construction of three floating batteries. These were to be flat-bottomed vessels carrying forts with iron walls four inches thick, pierced for broadside guns. In 1855, the lumbering structures were towed near a Russian fort on Kinburn Spit in the Black Sea. Then they were released to move to the attack under their own meager steam power, which allowed a top speed of two miles an hour.

Three hours later, the Russians surrendered. Their fort was in ruins. Most of their guns had been knocked out, and 175 men were dead. Aboard the floating batteries, two men were killed. The only external signs that the batteries had been in a fight were rust-streaked dents in their iron sides where shells had exploded harmlessly. Iron armor had proved invulnerable to shellfire. The ironclad ship showed it could demolish lesser structures and remain virtually unmolested itself.

France immediately started to build more ironclads. England shortly followed. In addition to floating batteries, which were somewhat similar to the Confederate *Virginia*, France built the *Gloire*, and England the *Warrior*. These were fast frigates with sails and steam, belted with iron armor. By the time the Civil War was a year old, the navies of the world were rapidly being complemented with ironclads - more than 100 had been launched or were being designed and constructed.

Secretary Welles realized the United States should not lag behind. An attempt to build an ironclad had been abandoned back in 1841 because Congress objected to the expense. Then, in August 1861, spurred on by the war, but as yet uncertain of the South's plans for the *Virginia,* Welles pushed a bill through Congress authorizing the U.S. Navy to spend $1.5 million to investigate and build one or more ironclad ships. It took only about two weeks for the bill to go from draft to President Lincoln's desk, where it was signed into law. Much of the credit for this quick turnaround belongs to a master lobbyist named Cornelius Bushnell.

Thirty-two-year-old Bushnell was an ambitious man with high-profile connections. Born in Connecticut, he had first demonstrated his drive as a teenager, becoming master of a sixty-ton schooner a year after starting an apprenticeship at sea. By age twenty-eight, he had made a small fortune running a grocery business with his brother Nathan. Then, in the spring of 1858, he bought a single share in the bankrupt New Haven & New London Railroad, and at a shareholder's meeting convinced the other investors to expand, rather than abandon, the line. Soon after successful completion of rail service from New York City to Boston, Bushnell was elected president of the railroad. In this position, he often had reason to be in Washington, where he met many important people while lobbying for government contracts to carry the mail.

He was in the nation's capital when the war broke out, and eager to serve, joined a temporary militia to defend it. Relieved of this duty with the arrival of the 6th Massachusetts Infantry, Bushnell soon found another way to contribute. One of his Washington contacts, Commodore Hiram Paulding – fresh from the disastrous abandonment of the Norfolk shipyard – suggested that the railroad man could give the Union a considerable advantage by building a ship of iron.

Bushnell wasted no time in pursuing an ironclad, quickly hiring a naval constructor from Boston named Samuel H. Pook. Over three months, the pair worked on a design that would become the *Galena* – a 210-foot, propeller-driven wooden steamer covered with iron bars. He took the design to Gideon Welles in early July, and over the course of their conversation, the Ironclads Bill was drafted. Bushnell called on his friends in Congress, including Connecticut Congressman James E. King, who sat on the House Naval Committee. By August 3, he was officially in the ironclads business.

The U.S. Navy Department sent notices to shipbuilders that it would consider ideas for armored vessels, listing specifications that were both meticulous and short-sighted. To be considered, a ship had to be capable of carrying eighty to 120 tons of armaments, sixty days' provisions, and eight days' of coal, while maintaining a draft of between ten and sixteen feet. A successful design, the Navy stated, would also include at least two masts with standard wire rigging. Sixteen proposals were submitted before the twenty-five-day deadline passed, including one for a "rubberclad" ship that was dismissed immediately – and Bushnell's *Galena*.

The choice fell to the newly created Ironclad Board, made up of Paulding, Commodore Joseph Smith, and Commander Charles Davis. Smith, a fifty-two-year veteran of the Navy, would oversee construction of the ironclads as chief of the Bureau of Yards and Docks. His son was Lieutenant Joseph B. Smith, the captain of the ill-fated USS *Congress* who would be killed in the Battle of Hampton Roads. Davis, who had served on the board that directed the blockade of Southern ports after the Battle of Fort Sumter, stepped in when the Navy's first choice, ordnance expert John Dahlgren, declined the appointment. The Ironclad Board dismissed some proposals on cost alone, deciding $1 million was too much to spend on a single ship. Skeptical that other designs would be stable enough to carry the weight of the iron, the board members finally settled on two: the *Galena* and the *New Ironsides*.

The *New Ironsides* was the most promising of the pair – and, in fact, would serve the Union well in bombardments of Confederate forts at Charleston, South Carolina, and Wilmington, North Carolina.

Designed by Philadelphia engine-builders Merrick & Sons, the *New Ironsides* copied many features of the French ship *La Gloire*. Her 220-foot-long wooden hull was covered in an armor of interlocking iron rails. Bulky by comparison, the *Galena* was given only provisional approval by the Ironsides Board, which required proof that it would indeed float before construction could begin. Cornelius Bushnell had already contracted with ironworks in Troy, New York, to press the *Galena's* armor. As he scrambled now to keep his project afloat, another late entry in the ironclad game would emerge.

Ericsson's Folly

The Navy did not request the services of the one man in the United States who knew more about building novel ships than anybody else, Captain John Ericsson. He was a Swedish engineer and an inventive genius who had built, among other things, the first steam-powered fire engine.

Born in 1803, John became a cadet of mechanics with the Swedish Royal Navy by age seven - along with his brother Nils, who was a year older. The brothers studied under Baltzar von Platen, architect of the Göta Canal, which their father worked to excavate. By age fourteen, John was working independently as a surveyor. After some time in the Swedish army, which promoted him to lieutenant at seventeen, he moved to England in 1826 to focus on engineering. His work to develop heat- and steam-powered engines landed him briefly in debtors' prison. He designed a two-screw-propeller, which was refused by the British Admiralty but caught the attention of an American Navy captain named Robert Stockton.

Stockton had Ericsson design a ship using his propeller and convinced him to sail it across the Atlantic in 1839 to New York, where he assured him there would be a better market for it. In New York, Ericsson met industrialist Cornelius DeLamater, who put him to work in the DeLamater Iron Works and funded his experimentations. Ericsson moved into a house at 95 Franklin Street, not far from the foundry, in lower Manhattan. Between 1840 and 1850, he built two small steamships and twenty-four other boats of various sizes, powered by his engines and propellers. But his biggest project, started shortly after his arrival in New York, was to build a propeller-driven steam warship for the U.S. Navy – a contract Stockton helped to secure.

The warship took nearly three years to complete, during which the relationship between Ericsson and Stockton grew increasingly tense, with Stockton trying to claim most of the credit. The USS *Princeton*, named for Stockton's New Jersey hometown, was built in the Philadelphia Navy Yard, and launched on September 5, 1843, to some fanfare. She sailed to Washington in early 1944, captained by Stockton, to perform in trials and demonstrations for eager politicians and military officials. The *Princeton* mastered most tests, including a race with British steamer SS *Great Western* which she won handily. But on February 28, something went terribly wrong.

About 400 distinguished guests were on board - including President John Tyler, his Cabinet, and former first lady Dolley Madison – for a pleasure cruise down the Potomac when one of the guests called for a demonstration of the *Princeton*'s firing power. The warship had been fitted with two experimental guns: the Oregon, a twelve-inch smooth bore muzzleloader designed by Ericsson; and the Peacemaker, built to Stockton's specifications in an attempt to emulate Ericsson's design. When fired, the Peacemaker exploded, spraying shrapnel into the crowd. Six people were killed, including Secretary of State Abel P. Upshur and Secretary of the Navy Thomas W. Gilmer; twenty others were injured.

Although he had not built the faulty weapon, the Navy blamed Ericsson for the accident and refused to pay him for his work on the ship. When the inventor appealed to Congress for relief, the Navy labeled him a troublemaker. His once friend and backer, Robert Stockton, helped sully his reputation. Later, Stockton would lead the criticism of his greatest innovation, labeling it "Ericsson's Folly." In 1861, he was still out of favor and considered a difficult man to get along with. Ericsson had vowed to never again work for the U.S. Navy, but his mind was changed by a visitor to his Franklin Street home.

Cornelius DeLamater had gone to Washington to offer his ironworks to Navy Secretary Gideon Welles for the ironclad project. There, he met Cornelius Bushnell at Willard's Hotel, where both men were staying. Bushnell confided to DeLamater that he had designed an ironclad, but had the problem of proving it seaworthy. DeLamater suggested that his man in New York, John Ericsson, "would settle the matter definitely and with accuracy," and the next day, Bushnell boarded a train heading north.

Ushered by a maid into an office that doubled as a bedroom, Bushnell saw the Swedish genius sitting on a revolving piano stool. Fifty-eight-years-old, Ericsson had a stern face, framed by large, bushy sideburns, that suggested he had no time or patience for nonsense. Bushnell got quickly to the point, saying that he had been sent by Ericsson's benefactor, and showing the plans that were the purpose of his visit. It was late in the afternoon, and Ericsson asked him to leave the plans and come back the next day.

When Bushnell returned, he found an invigorated adviser. From the pages of elaborate calculations he had devised, it seemed likely that Ericsson had stayed up all night working out an answer to Bushnell's question. He stated it simply, for

Bushnell's benefit: The *Galena* "will easily carry the load you propose, and stand a six-inch shot at a respectable distance." Bushnell was eager to take the good news back to Washington, but Ericsson stopped him. "Since you are interested in ironclads, you might like to see this," he said, showing him a cardboard model of a strange-looking little ship.

Ericsson explained that the model was an ironclad that he had tried to sell to the French eight years before. Napoleon III, busy with his floating batteries, had been impressed, and even awarded Ericsson a medal that he proudly displayed to Bushnell. But the French emperor ultimately turned down the design, which was deemed too expensive. It was, essentially, the *Monitor* - a name that Ericsson himself later gave his creation. He felt it would serve as an effective monitor, or reminder, to the South and to ambitious European powers of the Union's military strength. While the ironsides of Bushnell's *Galena* would resist shots fired at a distance, Ericsson assured him that the *Monitor* was "absolutely impervious to the heaviest shot or shell."

Bushnell excitedly took the model to Gideon Welles, who presented it to a Naval Committee for consideration. The model became the object of much argument. By now, it was late September 1861, and the deadline had long since passed for designs to be considered by the Ironclad Board. To sway the board to make an exception, Bushnell called on two business associates, John A. Griswold, president of the Troy City Bank, and iron-plate manufacturer John F. Winslow, and offered them a quarter interest each in the ironclad if Ericsson's design were awarded the contract. Together, the businessmen approached Ironclad Board member Commodore Joseph Smith, who was unimpressed. Even Abraham Lincoln became involved. When asked for his opinion, the president said, "All I can say is what the girl said when she put her foot in the stocking. 'It strikes me there's something in it.'"

Rumors of the Confederates' ironclad had begun to circulate; some stated she was almost finished. Ericsson said that he could build his ship in 100 days – a miracle of engineering if he could pull it off. Desperate for an ironclad to meet the Southern monster, the Navy ordered the *Monitor*. A small-print clause in the contract stated that if Ericsson did not meet his 100-day deadline, he would have to refund the Navy all of the cost. The ironclad was delivered in 101 days, which the Navy deemed acceptable, for a price of $275,000. In comparison, the *New Ironsides* took a little less than a year to build and cost the Navy $780,000. "The magnitude of the work I have to do," Ericsson said, "exceeds anything I have ever before undertaken."

Ericsson's ship was radically different from any previous vessel ever built. Its base was a conventional hull. Atop this was placed an iron-covered raft 172 feet long that formed a deck. Rising from the forward end of this was an iron pilothouse four feet high, built like a blockhouse. In the center of the raft was a cylindrical turret nine feet high and twenty feet in diameter, made of eight layers of one-inch iron plate. In the turret were two eleven-inch guns. An engine designed to revolve the turret like a merry-go-round was in the hull, along with another engine to propel the ship.

Smoke escaped from two gratings in the deck. Air for the crew and the fires was admitted to the hull through two other vents and then blown through the ship by a system of fans which Ericsson had devised. The deck of the *Monitor* was only a foot above water, and it was necessary to place portable square stacks over these four holes when the ship was ocean-going. The stacks could be removed when the vessel went into battle.

The turret was a bold innovation in warship design. For centuries, naval firing power had been based on broadside guns which could be aimed only a few degrees up and down or sideways. There was a saying that "the sailors aimed the ship and the gunners fired the guns." The *Monitor's* guns could fire in any direction regardless of the position of the ship, except directly over the bow, where the pilothouse blocked the way.

When Ericsson started to build the *Monitor* in October 1861, he entered a shipbuilding race in which the Southerners had a head start of more than three months. But the North had ample mills, shops, mechanics, and materials for the job. One company built the hull, another the turret, a third the engines. The DeLamater Iron Works, of course, manufactured the ship's major machinery, including boiler and turret-turning apparatus. Four mills rolled the iron armor. And, more important than men and materials, the North had John Ericsson. When he started, he had only a cardboard model. Detailed plans were needed. Every day, the tireless Swede moved from shipyard to machine shop to rolling mill, supervising the work. Every night, he spent hours at his drafting board designing the next steps and inventing many of the ship's features as he went along.

Construction of the ship was well in progress before Ericsson received the actual contract from the Navy to build it. He ignored the clause that someone in the Navy Department had inserted, saying that the *Monitor* should have masts and sails capable of moving her at a speed of six knots. The *Monitor* and the *Virginia* were both firsts in this respect - they were the first major warships without sails since the days of the rowed galleys.

Few people in the North or the South had much faith in the ironclads. On paper, so-called experts on both sides proved that neither ship would float with its great weight of armor. As was the case with the *Virginia,* security was lax at the New York factories, giving the public plenty of information from which to pass judgment. In mid-November 1861, the magazine *Scientific American* published details about the design of the *Monitor.* The ship that Robert Stockton called "Ericsson's Folly" was derided by others as the "Yankee cheesebox." Ericsson never wavered in his faith, though the U.S. Navy grew more anxious every day.

Commodore Joseph Smith, of the Ironclad Board, had his own informants among the *Monitor* builders, and their reports raised concerns. Smith did not like Ericsson and had fought his design from the start. This sentiment was shared by the Navy's chief engineer Benjamin Franklin Isherwood, who thought Ericsson an unreliable eccentric. It was likely Isherwood who sounded the alarm on such questions as the ship's ventilation ("Sailors do not fancy living under water without breathing in sunshine occasionally," Smith wrote to Ericsson), rudder design, and other particulars. Ericsson calmly replied to each inquiry, begging patience and giving reassurances, though he admitted to Smith: "It is an unpleasant task continually to contradict the opinions you express."

With the 100-day deadline approaching fast, Smith continued to pressure the designer. Problems at the various factories threatened to cause delays. The DeLamater plant had turned out a "somewhat peculiar" engine, even by Ericsson's standards, "consisting of only one steam cylinder with pistons at opposite ends, a steam tight partition being introduced in the middle. The propeller shaft has only one crank and one crank pin." Across Manhattan at the Novelty Ironworks, the massive turret was taking shape – nine feet high, with ironsides eight inches thick. But as big as the turret was, the builders were having trouble making room to accommodate both the recoil of the two eleven-inch Dahlgren guns and the crew (eight men to each gun).

To help seek solutions, Ericsson called on a Navy engineer named Albert C. Stimers, who coincidentally had served previously on the *Merrimac*. Stimers proved capable of operating the *Monitor*'s odd engine, but on the gun problem, his recommendation to simply shorten the barrels was dismissed. The gunmaker, Admiral John Dahlgren, said to do so would reduce the guns' effectiveness by half, and Smith would not allow it. Ericsson instead had wrought-iron crossbeams installed that acted as slides on which the gun carriages could run in and out. These slides would make it possible for one man to move the gun, and allow a maximum recoil of six feet. Friction mechanisms, similar to what Ericsson had designed for the *Princeton*, reduced the recoil even further - to as little as two feet.

On January 25, 1862, Northern spies reported that the Confederates had floated their iron battery out of dry dock, and Smith urged Ericsson to hold trials for the *Monitor* as soon as possible. Five days later, at 9:45 a.m. on January 30, the *Monitor* slipped down a ramp into the cold waters of the East River.

When the water was let into the *Virginia*'s dry dock, her officers stood prudently on the dock, not on the ship's deck. When the *Monitor* slid down the ways, Ericsson stood on the deck. In the crowd on shore, anybody who wanted to bet that it would float could get good odds, and a small boat stood by to pick up Ericsson when the ship went under. But both ships floated as planned.

The "highly successful launch" was reported in the next day's *Brooklyn Daily Eagle,* which described the *Monitor* as "broad and flat-bottomed, with vertical sides and pointed ends, requiring but a very small low depth of water to float in, though heavily loaded with impregnable armor upon its sides and a bomb-proof deck, on which is placed a shot-proof revolving turret, that will contain two very heavy guns."

This test meant little to the U.S. Navy, which would consider the *Monitor* a success only if she could stand up to Confederate guns. Failure in the initial battle would violate the contract, forcing Ericsson to refund all costs of building the ironclad. Commodore Smith stressed this requirement in a letter to Ericsson: "So soon as the vessel is ready for service the Government will send her on the coast and put her before the enemy's batteries in the service for which you intend her. No other test can be made to prove the vessel and her appointments than that to which both parties agree to expose her. . . . The plan is novel and because it is so, the Government requires the designer to warrant its success. Placing the vessel before an enemy's batteries will test its capacity to resist shot and shell – that is the least of the difficulties I apprehend in the success of the vessel, but it is one of the properties of the vessel which you set forth as of great merit. The Government cannot consent to receive the vessel until she shall have been tested in the manner proposed."

Secretary of the Navy Gideon Welles later confirmed the details of what would be the *Monitor*'s first mission: "When the contract for *Monitor* was made . . . the Navy Department intended that the battery should, immediately after reaching Hampton Roads, proceed up Elizabeth river to the Navy Yard at Norfolk, place herself opposite the dry-dock, and with her great guns destroy both the dock and the *Merrimac*. This was our secret."

Ericsson had overcome the Southerners' lead, but factors beyond his control soon plagued the project. There was a problem procuring guns for the *Monitor*; finally, on February 5, the Navy authorized an ordnance officer at the Brooklyn

Navy Yard to take two guns from the gunboat *Dacotah*. A few days later, there was an explosion in the blacksmith shop. Violent rain, wind, and snowstorms whipped the harbor, causing damage to several ships, but the *Monitor* was spared. The weather stopped short a trial on February 19 when it was discovered that steam valves had been installed backward so that the ship could not get up to speed. While adjustments were made, the *Virginia* neared completion.

The shipbuilding race ended in a dead heat. The *Monitor* was commissioned on February 25 at the Brooklyn Navy Yard – a week after the *Virginia* in Norfolk. Ericsson telegraphed Washington that his ironclad would depart the next day. But only a mile downstream, the *Monitor* had to turn back to correct some minor defects, principally with the rudder. Ericsson, annoyed by yet another delay, refused to let the ship be docked, and made the adjustment to the steering mechanism himself.

The crew of the *Monitor* – forty-nine volunteers and enlisted men and ten officers – waited. Just as irritated as Ericsson was the ship's captain, Lieutenant John L. Worden. He had arrived at the Brooklyn Navy Yard on January 16 to take command of the *Monitor*. A twenty-six-year Navy veteran, the forty-three-year-old lieutenant had no trouble recruiting men to serve aboard the *Monitor*, though he told them bluntly: "I won't draft any of you for service on that thing. I merely call for volunteers. I can't promise to get you to Hampton Roads, but if I ever do I think she will do good service." The men described Worden as tall, thin and "quite effeminate looking," though he had a tremendous beard that ended mid-chest. For Worden, the war had started badly.

In April 1861, Worden had been assigned to carry secret dispatches - regarding the reinforcement of Fort Pickens – south to warships at Pensacola, Florida. On his way back north, he was arrested by Confederates in Alabama, becoming one of the first prisoners of war. He was held for more than seven months before a prisoner exchange on November 20 sent him home. Not two months later, Worden received his orders from Commodore Smith, who wrote: "I have only time to say I have named you for the command of the battery under contract with Captain Ericsson, now nearly ready at New York. This vessel is an experiment. I believe you are the right sort of officer to put in command of her."

Worden was enthusiastic about the appointment, though his family and physicians urged him to decline it. He was still weak and ill from being held captive when he arrived in New York, and the delays in launching the *Monitor* had given him time to heal. But he was tired of waiting.

Ericsson was adamant that the *Monitor* would be ready in two days. Worden was not convinced the problem had been solved and demanded another trial, which was completed successfully on March 3. Then, for the first time, the guns were put to the test. A small oversight with the friction device caused one gun, when fired, to recoil terribly, slamming into the other side of the turret. But apart from startling the crew, no damage was done, and the problem was easily corrected. Two crew members deserted in the aftermath, taking the ship's cutter, and had to be replaced. At last, the *Monitor* was ready for war.

4
"OUR ONE CHANCE
IS THE MONITOR"

On March 6, 1862, Captain Buchanan of the *Virginia* told his officers that he would attack the next day. On the same day, the *Monitor* left New York for Hampton Roads at the end of a towline behind the steamer *Seth Low*. A storm delayed the *Virginia*'s attack for one day. The same storm almost sank the *Monitor*.

The morning had been cold but clear, and Lieutenant Worden sent a dispatch to Navy Secretary Welles stating the mission had begun in haste, "whilst the fine weather lasts." The moon reflected off of the calm, still water of the North Atlantic. Engineer Alban Stimers, who had volunteered to accompany the crew, reported that "there has not been sufficient movement to disturb a wine glass setting on the table." By dawn on March 7, the weather had changed.

The crew was woken by the whipping ocean waves, which tossed the heavy *Monitor* like she was a paper bag and spilled over her upper deck. The ship's hatches had not been properly sealed, and water gushed into the turret, engine room, and hull. The men were soaked and miserable, but the ship held up to hours of unrelenting storms. Then, under the rush of the water, blowers that kept the ship's boilers lit began to fail. The same belts that turned the ventilation fans had slipped and stretched.

Twenty-two-year-old Lieutenant Samuel D. Greene, executive officer of the *Monitor*, wrote his mother a long letter which contains the best description of the storms that came close to depriving the North of its ironclad even before it had been in battle:

> I turned out at six o'clock on Friday morning and from that time until Monday at 7 p.m. I think I lived ten good years. About noon the wind freshened and the sea was rough. In the afternoon the sea was breaking over our decks at a great rate and coming in our hawse pipe forward [the hole through which the anchor chain passed] in perfect floods . . . and the water came down under the tower like a waterfall. At 4 p.m. the water had gone down our smoke stacks and blowers to such an extent that the blowers

gave out and the engine room filled with gas. Then, Mother, Occurred a scene I shall never forget. Our engineers behaved like heroes, everyone of them. They fought with the gas, endeavoring to get the blowers to work until they dropped down as apparently dead as men ever were.

I jumped in the engine room with my men as soon as I could and carried them to the top of the tower to get fresh air. I was nearly suffocated with the gas myself but got on deck after everyone was out of the engine room, just in time to save myself.

We had no fear as long as the engine could be kept going to pump out the water, but when that stopped, the water increased rapidly.

The *Monitor*, filled with steam and choking gas, was on the point of foundering when, suddenly, the sea moderated. Worden had managed to signal the tug *Seth Low,* 400 feet ahead, to tow the *Monitor* closer to the land, where the water was calmer. The wet belts attached to the fans were dried out, the engine was started, the big steam-driven pump went to work, and the vessel was saved.

Lieutenant Greene described another narrow escape late Friday night when he was "startled by the most infernal noise I ever heard in my life . . . . The sea suddenly became rough right ahead. It came up with tremendous force, through our anchor well, and forced the air through our hawse pipe where the chain comes . . . We tried to hail the tug boat but the wind being dead ahead, they could not hear us. . . . From 4 a.m. till daylight was certainly the longest hour and a half I ever spent. . . . At last, however, we could see, and made the tug boat understand to go nearer to shore and get in smooth water."

After these two narrow escapes, the *Monitor* arrived at the mouth of Chesapeake Bay. A passing pilot boat told them of the fate of the *Congress* and the *Cumberland* at the hands of the *Virginia*. Lieutenant Worden, the *Monitor's* commander, signaled the tug for more speed, but it was dusk before his ship coasted past Fort Monroe, cast off her towline, and steamed into the Roads under her own power to anchor for the night.

In the distance, the *Virginia* could be faintly seen in the glare of the burning *Congress*; otherwise, except for the *Minnesota*, the upper end of Hampton Roads was deserted. The *Monitor* followed the flames, illuminating the water like a beacon, to anchor beside the towering *Minnesota*, whose captain, G. J. Van Brunt, was trying desperately to free her from the muddy bank. Lieutenant Worden went aboard the frigate to ask if the *Monitor* could help, but all the ironclad could offer was protection from the Confederate monster. That was enough;

Captain Van Brunt wrote that "all on board felt that we had a friend that would stand by us in our hour of trial." The fifty-nine men of the *Minnesota's* weary crew lined the top of the *Monitor's* turret to watch the *Congress* burn.

The fire so far had been limited to the gun and berth decks, and the survivors of the *Congress* were able to go above and prepare to evacuate. They used bits of cloth and sail to plug a few holes in the cutters made by flying shrapnel, and crammed onto the boats. When these makeshift patches failed, and the boats started to fill with water, the officers jumped out to lighten the load and swam the rest of the way. In all, thirty wounded men were taken ashore, along with the body of their captain, thirty-five-year-old Joseph Smith.

Up the bay, the crew of the *Virginia* also stared at the flames, as did 20,000 soldiers, blue and gray, from opposite shores. At midnight, the fire reached the magazine of the *Congress*, and she burst into a mushroom of flame. Burning timbers and sparks from the exploding ammunition shot high in the air and rained down on the dark water. The *Virginia's* engineer, H. Ashton Ramsay, described: "The magazines exploded, shooting up a huge column of firebrands hundreds of feet into the air, and then the burning hull burst asunder and melted into the waters, while the calm night spread her sable mantle over Hampton Roads." Lieutenant Greene, on the

Monitor, recalled: "A grander sight was never seen, but it went straight to the marrow of our bones." What was left of the *Congress* sank to a watery grave.

Dark stillness settled on the Roads. The men of the *Virginia* stretched out on the gun deck in exhausted sleep. The men of the *Monitor* went below to prepare their ship for the great battle of the morrow - the first battle of the ironclads.

David and Goliath

"Man your guns. Block your harbors. The *Merrimac* is coming." So read the telegrams that Northern Secretary of War Edwin Stanton sent to governors of the seacoast states on the morning of March 9, 1862. At an emergency Cabinet meeting, the excitable secretary described the awful fate of Washington if the Southern monster should come steaming up the Potomac.

Panic gripped Northern seaports at the thought of a visit from the *Virginia*. Philadelphians envisioned Independence Hall in ruins; New Yorkers saw the Stock Exchange in flames; Bostonians feared for historic North Church. Stanton ordered that barges be loaded with rocks and made ready to block the channel of the Potomac. New York sent barge-loads of coal down the bay to block the Narrows, and hastily summoned artillery units from upstate to help defend the city. Newport, Rhode Island, held a meeting to decide how to answer the commander of the *Virginia* when he demanded the surrender of the city.

Actually these fears were groundless. The *Virginia* was not a seagoing ship. Even the smallest waves of a quiet sea would have poured quantities of water through her low gun ports - if her sluggish engines lasted long enough to get her across Chesapeake Bay.

The calmest man in the Cabinet was Gideon Welles. He read a telegram to the men assembled for the meeting: "I have the honor to report that I have arrived at this anchorage at nine o'clock this evening and am ordered to proceed immediately to the assistance of the *Minnesota* aground near Newport News." The message was sent from Hampton Roads by Lieutenant Worden, commander of the *Monitor*. This provoked another hysterical outburst from Stanton. If all that the Navy had to pit against the Southern monster was "Ericsson's Folly" with its two puny guns, the Union was lost indeed. Nobody listened to Gideon Welles when he said, "Our one hope, our one chance, is the *Monitor*."

At Hampton Roads, the Confederate soldiers-turned-sailors awoke and readied the *Virginia* for the day's battle. Rumors spread about a strange craft that was moored beside the *Minnesota*. Some thought it was a water tank, others believed it was a raft that had come to take the crew off the doomed vessel. Later, some said it looked like a "tin can on a shingle," others compared it to a "cheese box on a raft." Except for Worden and his men, few people in the North or the South considered the little ship a dangerous adversary for the mighty *Virginia*. The captain of a tugboat struggling to free the *Minnesota* said, "What can that little thing do? We could lick her ourselves."

The two ironclads have always been compared to David and Goliath. Actually the *Monitor*, although smaller, had many advantages over the Southern ship. She was faster - seven miles an hour to the *Virginia's* five. She drew ten feet of water to the *Virginia's*, twenty-two, and she was a hard target. The little pilothouse and the turret were all that rose above the water. The *Virginia* had ten guns, but she could never use more than four at one time, and when she was not in position to use her broadsides, she could use only one gun - either her bow or her stern gun. The *Monitor* was able to fire her two guns from almost any position, except when she was pointed head-on at a target. And, the bore of her guns had a diameter of eleven inches, whereas the largest gun on the *Virginia* measured only nine inches in diameter.

All along the shoreline of Hampton Roads, soldiers and civilians crowded to watch the ironclads battle, creating a scene "suggestive of the greatest performance ever given in the largest theater ever seen," noted one Southerner.

Black smoke belched from the *Virginia's* stack as she started her slow-motion approach toward the *Minnesota*. It was 6:00 a.m. aboard the *Monitor;* the crew munched on their breakfast of dry ship's biscuit and waited. An hour and a half passed before the creeping monster came within firing range of the frigate and her tiny defender. The bow gun of the *Virginia* and the stern gun of the *Minnesota* spoke almost in unison to open the battle. The little Yankee ironclad moved forward, looking rather like a small dog rushing to defend a tall stag from a lumbering bear.

The *Virginia* pivoted her bow gun to fire at the *Monitor* - and missed. The little ship came on silently. She could not fire as she approached without shooting away her own pilothouse. At close range, she turned sharply and coasted past the side of the Southerner. Her solid shot glanced off the *Virginia's* sloping side. The *Virginia's* broadside guns fired. When the smoke cleared, the Union watchers gave a mighty cheer. The Confederate shells had exploded harmlessly against the turret.

After the first exchange, Lieutenant Worden dropped down out of the pilothouse, ran back below deck, and climbed into the turret. Experts had predicted that the explosion of shells against the turret's side would break off the heads of the bolts joining the layers of iron and send them flying about the turret like musket balls. The experts were wrong. Worden next tried the lever that made the turret revolve and was greatly relieved when it turned smoothly. The experts were again wrong when they predicted that jarring explosions would jam the turret mechanism.

The lieutenant dropped through one of the gun ports and ran across the exposed deck. A shell had hit the edge of the deck where the raft joined the hull. The same experts had said that this was a weak point. Again they were mistaken. Worden dodged exploding shells and Confederate snipers' bullets as he dashed back from the turret to the pilothouse. He had learned what Buchanan had found out the day before - there was not a gun in Hampton Roads that could hurt an ironclad.

For the next three hours, the battle was a noisy and awkward waltz. The cumbersome *Virginia* slowly turned in an effort to bring her broadside guns to bear on the elusive *Monitor*. The faster Yankee ship darted around her, seeking a vantage point at the bow or stern. Aboard the *Virginia*, Lieutenant Catesby Jones longed for the solid steel projectiles that were lying on the dock at Norfolk. They might have penetrated the *Monitor's* armor.

On the *Monitor*, Lieutenant Worden fumed at the Navy Department's order that kept him from using more than fifteen pounds of powder in his guns. The new weapons had not been tested for a heavier charge. Later, it was learned that these guns could be fired safely with thirty pounds. Had Worden disobeyed his orders and double-charged his guns, his solid projectiles might have broken the *Virginia's* iron skin.

Lieutenant Greene, in command of the *Monitor's* turret, found that his firepower was less effective than it might have been because of a serious, but unforeseen, design defect. The gun ports had heavy iron shutters which were closed when the muzzle-loading guns were drawn in to be recharged. When they were closed, Greene could not see out, and he lost his sense of direction in the spinning turret. From the pilothouse, Lieutenant Worden relayed such messages to him as "I'm going to bring her on our starboard beam close alongside." This was not much help to Greene, who in his enclosed merry-go-round, could not tell port from starboard or bow from stern. All he could do was open the shutters when the guns were loaded, run them out, spin the turret, and fire on the fly when his opponent came in view. Eventually, the turret was simply kept stationary, and the whole ship was pointed to aim the guns.

For much of the battle, the ships were within a range of ten yards. Most of the time, clouds of smoke wreathed the contestants, and the clang of shells against turret and casemate sounded like a devil's anvil chorus. Every time the smoke drifted away, the hopes of Union watchers on shore rose higher as they saw their little champion darting around her opponent, still unharmed.

The *Virginia* fired whenever a gun would bear, but the midget *Monitor* was hard to hit - and when she was hit, nothing happened. As the morning progressed, Confederate Lieutenant Jones came down to the gun deck and found a gun crew standing idle. When he asked why, the officer in charge said, "Our powder is precious, and after two hours of incessant firing, I find that I can do as much damage . . . snapping my thumb at her every two minutes and a half."

After three hours, the *Monitor* broke off the fight and ran into shallow water to replenish the ammunition in her turret. The *Virginia*, unable to follow her, turned toward the *Minnesota*. Captain Van Brunt, commanding the big frigate, fired his broadside at the Southern ship. He later said that this fire would have "blasted any wooden ship in the world out of the water." But the *Virginia* was unharmed.

Lieutenant Jones, seeing the *Monitor* returning to the battle and knowing that his guns could not hurt the little ship, decided to ram her. Even without the iron ram, he reasoned that the great weight of the monster must drive the pygmy under. Jones rang for full speed and lumbered forward. The agile *Monitor* swerved so that she received only a harmless, glancing blow. As the ships parted, Greene fired two 168-pound solid projectiles against the front of the *Virginia*'s casemate from a few feet away. The outer iron cracked, and the men at the forward gun were sent spinning across the deck by the shock, but no one was seriously hurt.

The *Virginia*'s rush at the *Monitor* carried her out of the narrow channel. Her bow lodged firmly in the mud. As the Confederates struggled to free their ship, the Yankee vessel took a position off her stern and blasted her, without effect, for half an hour. Lieutenant Jones, meanwhile, ordered the safety valves on the *Virginia*'s boilers tied down, and the furnaces fed with oily rags to increase steam pressure. The flailing propeller churned through the mud and finally pulled her loose.

Now Lieutenant Worden on the *Monitor* sought another method of disabling the *Virginia*. The Southern ship's rudder was protected only by the wooden deck. If he could hit the *Virginia* in the center of the stern, he might damage the rudder and make the ship unmanageable. He tried, but his shot missed by a few feet.

As the ships passed close together, the captain of the *Virginia*'s stern gun took careful aim and placed a shell against the eye slit of the *Monitor*'s pilothouse. Flame and powder grains flashed into Worden's eyes. The explosion also blew off the metal plate that covered the pilothouse. For an instant, as the sunlight streamed into Worden's face, he thought that the pilothouse had been demolished. He called to the helmsman to sheer off and then staggered down the ladder to the deck below.

Word was passed to Lieutenant Greene in the turret. He found his commander clinging to the pilothouse ladder, his face a mask of blood. With the surgeon's assistance, he helped Worden to his cabin and hastened to the pilothouse to take command. While this was happening, the *Monitor* had been wandering aimlessly away from the battle site, toward Fort Monroe. Greene ordered the helmsman to bring her about and return to the battle.

The Confederates were elated when they saw the *Monitor* leave the fight. They thought the day was theirs. Aboard the *Minnesota*, the Yankees were dismayed. Their hopelessly grounded ship was now at the mercy of the monster. They had learned that their guns were useless against the ironclad, and besides, they were almost out of ammunition. During the two-day battle, the *Minnesota* had fired 145 ten-inch rounds, 349 nine-inch rounds, thirty-five eight-inch shells, and more than 5,500 pounds of gunpowder. Three of her crew had been killed, and sixteen wounded. Captain Van Brunt gave orders for turpentine-soaked wood shavings to be piled against the mast and a powder train laid to the magazine. When the *Virginia* attacked, he planned to burn his ship rather than have her captured.

However, when Lieutenant Jones ordered his pilots to steer the *Virginia* closer to the frigate, they told him it was impossible - the water was too shallow. Also, they told him that with the falling tide, the *Virginia* would be stranded in the Roads if she did not return to the river mouth immediately.

Jones called a conference of the officers. The ship could still fight, but she had taken a beating. The muzzles of two guns had been blown off. The smokestack was gone, and without a draft, steam could barely be kept up in the boilers. She was leaking at the bow where she had glanced off the *Monitor* in her attempt to ram. The *Virginia* could not destroy the *Minnesota* from that distance, and there was nothing else to fight. The officers decided to return to Norfolk for repairs - and to get the steel projectiles that might damage the *Monitor* in a future fight.

The *Virginia* crept away slowly, as Jones looked back longingly at the helpless frigate that they had been trying to destroy for two days. He did not know that had he stayed a few minutes longer, Van Brunt would have done the job for him.

When the *Monitor* returned to the battle site, her crew saw the *Virginia* limping away. Now *they* had nothing to fight. The battle was over.

It had been a strange engagement. The ships had fought for hours at point-blank range, but nobody was killed; only Worden was seriously hurt, and neither ship was badly damaged. The *Monitor* had been struck twenty-two times, including nine hits to the turret and two to the pilothouse. Ninety-seven shells, meanwhile, had dented the *Virginia*; Lieutenant Catesby Jones described the condition of the Confederate ironclad in his official report: "Our loss is 2 killed and 19 wounded. The stem is twisted and the ship leaks. We have lost the prow, starboard anchor, and all the boats. The armor is somewhat damaged; the steam muzzles of two of the guns shot away. It was not easy to keep a flag flying. The flagstaffs were repeatedly shot away. The colors were hoisted to the smokestack and several times cut down from it."

For years, North and South would argue about who had won, each side claiming victory on the grounds that the other had been the first to leave the scene. Confederate Secretary of the Navy Stephen Mallory's report to President Jefferson Davis expressed no doubt in the outcome: "The conduct of the Officers and men of the squadron . . . reflects unfading honor upon themselves and upon the Navy. The report will be read with deep interest and its details will not fail to rouse the ardor and nerve the arms of our gallant seamen. It will be remembered that the *Virginia* was a novelty in naval architecture, wholly unlike any ship that ever floated; that her heaviest guns were equal novelties in ordnance; that her motive power and obedience to her helm were untried; and her officers and crew strangers comparatively, to the ship and to each other; and yet, under all these disadvantages, the dashing courage and consummate professional ability of Flag Officer Buchanan and his associates achieved the most remarkable victory which naval annals record."

Still, Lieutenant Jones's command was criticized, primarily for his failure to finish the grounded *Minnesota*, and he retired under pressure. When, more than a year later, the Confederate Navy offered a promotion to commander for "gallant and meritorious conduct as executive and ordnance officer of the steamer *Virginia* in the action at Hampton Roads on the 8th of March, 1862," the bitter Jones nearly turned it down.

The North unquestionably achieved one important goal - the *Monitor* had succeeded in preventing the *Virginia* from destroying the rest of the fleet in the Roads. As U.S. Secretary of the Navy Gideon Welles put it: "There is no reason to believe that any of our wooden vessels guarding the Southern Coast would have withstood [the *Virginia*'s] attacks any better than the *Cumberland*, *Congress*, or *Minnesota*. She might have ascended the Potomac, and thrown bombshells into the Capitol of the Union. In short, it is difficult to assign limits to her destructive power. But for the timely arrival of the *Monitor* . . . our whole fleet of wooden ships, and probably the whole sea coast, would have been at the mercy of a terrible assailant."

The crewmen of the *Monitor* were hailed as heroes. Assistant Secretary of the Navy Gustavus Fox, who had watched the battle from aboard the *Minnesota*, joked to the officers on the *Monitor*: "Well gentlemen, you don't look as though you just went through one of the greatest naval conflicts on record." But her captain, John Worden, never fully recovered. He was unconscious for three months while convalescing at his summer home in New York. Then, promoted to commander, he returned to captain another ironclad for the U.S. Navy, the *Montauk*, which would take part in the attack on Charleston, South Carolina, in April 1863. For the rest of the war and beyond, he would help direct construction in New York of the Navy's new ironclads, for which there was now a fervent need.

Beyond the immediate military significance of the encounter, the duel at Hampton Roads gained worldwide attention because it was the first clash between ironclads. Nobody had been sure what would happen when ironclad met ironclad. Now they knew. Against the naval weapons of the day - even against each other - ironclads were invincible.

5

"THEIR GALLANT SHIP
WAS NO MORE"

On the day after the great ironclad battle, President Lincoln asked Secretary Welles to relay this order: "It is directed by the president that the *Monitor* be not too much exposed; that under no event shall any attempt be made to proceed with her unattended to Norfolk." He had a good reason. General McClellan was preparing to attack Richmond by the back door - moving his army by water to Fort Monroe, and marching up the peninsula from there to take the Confederate capital from the southeast. If anything should happen to the *Monitor*, the thought of what the *Virginia* could do to McClellan's wooden troop transports was blood chilling.

As a result of the president's order, the ironclads never fought again. During the days and weeks after the fight, the *Monitor* simply waited at Fort Monroe. The *Virginia* returned to the shipyard at Norfolk, where the crew frantically bailed water as tugboats hefted her into dry dock for repairs.

The Confederate States Navy put every effort into restoring the *Virginia*. At the shipyard, the work never stopped, night and day. Still, Secretary of the Navy Stephen Mallory was anxious; eleven days after the ironclad went into dry dock, he wrote to Flag Officer French Forrest at the yard: "The work of getting the *Virginia* . . . ready for sea at the earliest possible moment is the most important duty that could devolve upon a naval officer at this time, and yet this Department is ignorant of what progress is being made. . . . I am not advised that a day's work has been done upon the *Virginia* since she went into dock."

Mallory had acted quickly to ensure that, this time, the *Virginia* would not be delayed by a lack of material. Within an hour of receiving reports of the Battle of Hampton Roads, the secretary had ordered the ironworks at Richmond to supply eight tons of rolled iron for the anticipated repairs. The iron was ready by March 10, and before the month was out, new plates had taken the place of damaged ones. A deeper and longer armored belt was installed around the hull's waterline, and a bigger ram mounted on the bow.

Southern newspapers began to speculate about what the *Virginia* would do next; the public, and even Secretary Mallory, got caught up in the infectious optimism. Mallory wrote to Captain Buchanan, still recovering in a hospital, to ask about the possibility of an attack on New York. "Such an event would eclipse all the glories of the combats on the sea . . . and would strike a blow from which the enemy would never recover," he wrote. "Peace would inevitably follow." The captain cautioned restraint: "The *Virginia* is yet an experiment and by no means invincible." Buchanan thought the ironclad would better serve in protection of Norfolk, but Mallory remained eager to put her out to sea.

In New York, the *Monitor*'s designer, John Ericsson, shared in her glory. Engineer Alban Stimers wrote to Ericsson from Fort Monroe: "You can form no idea of how very grateful the thousands of people here are to you for having produced this vessel." Ericsson was disappointed that the battle had not been more decisive. In a speech to the New York Chamber of Commerce, Ericsson praised Stimers as the "mastermind" behind the ironclad's success: "The men were new; their passage had been very rough, and the master had to put his vessel right under the heaviest guns that were ever worked on shipboard. It is evident that but for the presence of a mastermind on board of that vessel, that success could not have been achieved. Captain Worden, no doubt, acquitted himself in the most masterly manner. But everything was quite new.

He felt quite nervous before he went on board. The fact that the bulwark of the vessel was but one foot above the water-line was enough to make him so. When I was before the Naval Committee the grand objection was that in sea-way the vessel would not work. . . ."

Ericsson's comments did not go over well with the U.S. Navy, which had already given the credit to Captain Worden. But, considering the *Monitor's* trial a success, the Navy paid the balance of what it owed for the construction. Ericsson continued to design ships and weapons for the Navy, including a type of torpedo boat, christened the USS *Ericsson*, in 1890.

President Lincoln visited the bedridden Worden at his New York home to express the nation's gratitude, and got an earful from the captain about the *Monitor's* vulnerabilities. Some of the problems were already being addressed at the Brooklyn Navy Yard. Engineer Stimers designed reinforcements for the pilothouse to mimic the sloped casemate of the Confederate ironclad. Angled oak walls were built around the square pilothouse, covered with three one-inch layers of iron plate smeared with tallow and black lead so that enemy fire would glance off.

The Union Navy Department was flooded with ideas for coping with the cannon-proof Southern vessel, on the assumption that the ironclads would meet again. One suggestion was to put a derrick on the *Monitor* which could drop a two-ton weight on the *Virginia*'s deck. Another was a design for a machine that had a huge claw to hold the *Virginia* while a giant hammer beat her to pieces. One man advised using glass bullets filled with sulphuric acid that would eat holes in the Confederate ship's iron sides. Someone else proposed spraying the sides of the *Virginia* with pitch and then shooting balls of burning cotton against them, thus turning the ship into a vast oven. Many people had ideas for pouring things down the smokestack - boiling water, burning benzine, even chloroform. But they neglected to mention how they would get to the top of the tall stack.

The War Department had a more practical plan. The offer of a large ocean-going ship was accepted, and the steamer was sent to Hampton Roads to ram the *Virginia* when she next came out.

The South had its own ideas about handling the *Monitor*. Confederate naval experts reasoned that the Union ironclad, with her low deck, could be boarded easily. So groups of men were trained in commando boarding tactics. One party was to rush on board and throw a wet sail over the pilothouse to blind the ship. Another was equipped with wedges to drive under the *Monitor*'s gun turret. A third planned to pour benzine down the ventilating holes and set the interior of the ship on fire.

On April 11, 1862, the *Virginia* came back down the river and into Hampton Roads, accompanied by gunboats carrying the raiding party. The *Monitor* and the big ramming steamer hovered under the protecting guns of Fort Monroe. Lieutenant Jeffers had instructions not to attack the *Virginia* again unless the Southern ironclad went after any of the wooden ships. The *Virginia* cruised around for a while, surveying the situation. Confederates took possession of three small merchant ships that had run aground and towed them away with their Union flags inverted. But their taunts failed to draw out the *Monitor*. As the sun was setting, the *Virginia* fired a long-range shot at the Union ironclad that missed, and then steamed back to Norfolk.

Hundreds of Northerners, who again had gathered on the shoreline to witness the rematch of the ironclads, dispersed in disappointment. The *New York Herald* reported: "The public are very justly indignant at the conduct of our navy in Hampton Roads last Friday. . . . The wretched imbecility of the management of the Navy Department has paralyzed the best sailors and the best navy in the world."

Early in May, President Lincoln traveled to Hampton Roads to witness the *Monitor* and other ships attacking the Confederate land batteries at Sewell's Point, at the mouth of the Elizabeth River. The Southern ironclad came steaming down to attack on May 8, and the *Monitor* was ordered to withdraw.

There was a stalemate in the Roads - but the end of the *Virginia* was near.

Union General George B. McClellan was advancing into Virginia and, in so doing, cutting Norfolk off from the rest of the Confederacy. On the morning of May 10, the crew of the Southern ship awoke to find the Stars and Bars missing from its place above the shore batteries and to see flames spreading through the navy yard. The Confederates had evacuated Norfolk, setting the shipyard ablaze on their way out – just as the federals had the year before. The *Virginia* had no home base.

The newly appointed captain of the vessel, Josiah Tattnall, decided to attempt taking her up the James River to help defend Richmond. The pilots told him this could be done if the draft were decreased to eighteen feet. All day, the crew labored to throw ballast and coal overboard. Unloading as much as 600 tons of coal, the *Virginia*'s draft had been reduced by three feet. Then the pilots changed their minds and said that a shift in the wind had made the river too shallow. Tattnall suspected the pilots had deceived him, that their intentions all along had been to avoid battle.

Tattnall faced a difficult choice. His ship was now only partly armored; with the lightened load, the wooden hull was out of the water several feet. A single shot at this vulnerable area could sink her. It would be suicide to take her out, especially with the *Monitor* around. Rather than lose both ship and crew, he decided to destroy the ship and save the crew. Oil-soaked rags and powder trains were spread throughout the ship. All night long, the crew was ferried ashore in the *Virginia*'s two boats.

The fire was started. The crew stood on the shore and sadly watched the ship smolder, little tongues of flame flicking through the portholes. Then, at dawn, her magazine exploded with a mighty roar, sending chunks of iron and heavy timbers hurtling skyward. The crew silently turned their backs on the wreckage and started the march toward Richmond. Engineer H. Ashton Ramsay wrote: "The slow match, the magazine, and that last deep, low, sullen, mournful boom told our people, now far away on the march, that their gallant ship was no more."

A Confederate court of inquiry later would rule that "the destruction of the *Virginia* was ... unnecessary at the time and place it was effected," and that Tattnall was to blame for failing to use the ironclad in defense of the James River. Tattnall, though, demanded a court-martial, which after lengthy testimony acquitted him honorably.

"Send in the *Monitor*!"

Command of the *Monitor* changed hands four times between May and September 1862. Twenty-three-year-old Samuel Greene – mostly because of his "extreme youth," according to

Assistant Secretary of the Navy Fox – was relieved by Lieutenant Thomas O. Selfridge. Previously, Selfridge had captained the *Cumberland,* sunk on the first day of the Battle of Hampton Roads. His appointment was only meant to be temporary, and in fact only lasted two days. Lieutenant William Nichols Jeffers took over on May 15 and held the command for three months. The *Monitor* crew held out hope that Captain Worden would return, though he never did. Together, the men composed a letter:

DEAR SIR These few lines is from your own Crew of the *Monitor* with their Kindest Love to you there Honered Captain Hoping to God that they will have the pleasure of Welcoming you Back to us again Soon for we are all Ready able and willing to meet Death or any thing else only gives us Back our own Captain again Dear Captain we have got your Pilot house fixed and all Ready for you when you get well again and we all Sincerely hope that soon we will have the pleasure of welcoming you Back to it again (for since you left us we have had no pleasure on Board of the *Monitor* we once was happy on Board of our little *Monitor* But since we Lost you we have Lost our all that was Dear to us Still) . . . We Remain untill Death your Affectionate Crew, the Monitors Boys.

The light duty and the waiting had worn on the crew. Newspapers in Norfolk had criticized the *Monitor* for avoiding battle, and the men bristled at being called cowards. They were disappointed that their adversary, the *Virginia*, had fallen by her own hands. But with the *Virginia* destroyed, the *Monitor* boys soon would be back in the fight.

The *Monitor* was now freed from guarding the blockade fleet and the supply ships for McClellan's campaign against Richmond. With this powerful weapon available for action, the Navy adopted a bold plan to give naval support to McClellan, whose advance had stalled. The *Monitor,* accompanied by the new ironclad *Galena* and three gunboats, was sent up the James River to bombard the Southern capital.

Eight miles below Richmond, the James bends and narrows. Here the Confederates had sunk wooden hulks to block the channel and had built an earthwork, called Fort Darling, on Drury's Bluff commanding the bend. The Union ships could not get past without removing the hulks, and to do this they had to silence the heavy guns of Fort Darling. They took position close under the bluff and opened fire. The *Monitor's* guns could not be elevated enough to hit the fort 200 feet above, so she moved down the river about 1,000 yards. The plunging fire from the bluff soon put one gunboat out of action and forced the others to fall back to the *Monitor*, leaving the *Galena* to carry on the battle singlehandedly.

The *Galena* was a screw steamer mounting six guns and armored along the water line and amidships with about four inches of iron. She was, an officer said, "a most miserable contrivance . . . a poor stick of an ironclad." But, weak as she was, she tried. Marine Corporal John Mackie, on board the *Galena*, later gave this account of the battle:

> About eleven o'clock Fort Darling was re-enforced by the *[Virginia]* crew which was sent down from Richmond. They sprang upon the parapets and gave three cheers. We were so close to them that we could see the stripes of their uniforms.
>
> They then sprang to their guns and reopened fire on the fleet, particularly the *Galena*, smashing every one of our six small boats, cutting so many holes in our smokestacks that it reminded one of a nutmeg grater, tearing great gaps in our spar deck . . . . The ship began to fly all to pieces and in a short time we were a complete wreck. But no officer or man flinched from his duty, and our work went bravely on . . .
>
> As the gunner turned to go below an eight-inch solid shell pierced the port side,

killing him and four other men instantly and wounding several. This was followed almost within a moment by another eight-inch solid shot hitting a little farther forward, killing and wounding six men. After this came a shell which exploded on our deck, killing and wounding several men. . . .

Death and destruction reigned supreme for about ten minutes. Everybody believed the ship was on fire. As soon as the smoke cleared away a terrible sight was revealed to my eyes; the entire after division was down and the deck covered with dead and dying men. Without losing a moment, however, I called out to the men that there was a chance for them. I ordered them to clear away the dead and wounded and get the guns in shape. Splinters were swept from the guns, sand thrown on the deck which was slippery with human blood, and in an instant the heavy 100 pounder Parrott rifle and the two nine-inch Dahlgren guns were ready and at work upon the fort. Our first shots blew up one of the casemates and dismounted one of the guns that had been destroying the ship. . . .

At this time Captain Rogers was signaling to the fleet below when a shot cut the signal halyards, throwing them down on the deck and leaving a white signal flying at the fore. The signal quartermaster, Jeremiah Regan, saw the situation at a glance, sprang into the forerigging and climbed aloft under a heavy fire from the sharpshooters on the bank. He cleared the halyards, threw the white signal flag overboard, and then slid down the backstay and returned to his position unhurt. When asked by Captain Rogers why he threw the white signal flag overboard, he replied. "I wanted to show those rebels that we had no use for a white flag!" This was the spirit that animated the crew of the *Galena*.

But spirit was not enough. The *Galena's* armor was simply not adequate for the assignment. In fact, the effect of the bombardment from the fort was made more deadly by fragments broken off the ship's armor by the shells and solid shot. With steel flying throughout the ship, the crew was fortunate to have any survivors.

This time there was no doubt of the victory. The riddled *Galena* was forced to withdraw, and the Union vessels steamed back down the James. The army at Fort Darling, including the crew of the *Virginia*, had driven off two Union ironclads and, perhaps, saved their country's capital.

The *Monitor* stayed in the lower James throughout the summer. While the duty was not dangerous, it was not pleasant either. The hot Virginia sun beating down on the iron plates turned the ship into an oven. The temperature below deck reached 160 degrees; in the turret, it was equally hot. Flies infested the ship's iron hull, driving the crew mad. The men rejoiced when, in October, their ship was ordered to the Washington Navy Yard for repairs. Lying in the Potomac, she proudly displayed the dents in her armor to a steady swarm of admiring visitors, including President Lincoln.

The *Monitor* had also gone through two more captains. Commander Thomas H. Stevens, who replaced Lieutenant Jeffers in August, was much better liked. William F. Keeler, acting paymaster on the *Monitor,* wrote to his wife about the change: "I can assure you, we parted from [Jeffers] without many regrets. He is a person of a good deal of scientific attainment, but brutal, selfish & ambitious." Stevens held the command only a month, before passing the *Monitor* to her final captain, Lieutenant John Payne Bankhead.

The son of a brigadier general, Bankhead had been born at Fort Johnson on James Island, South Carolina, and his family was also prominent in Virginia. Like many, his family was divided by the war. He had two brothers; one had joined the Union Army as a regular officer, and the other was colonel in the Confederate Army. Bankhead was a twenty-four-year veteran of the U.S. Navy, having joined in 1838 at age seventeen and served under his father during the Mexican-American War. Before being assigned to the *Monitor,* he had bombarded the Confederate forts guarding Cape Hatteras, North Carolina, aboard the side-wheel steamer USS *Susquehanna,* and blockaded Charleston, South Carolina, with the gunboat *Pembina.* Now, at the Washington Navy Yard, he inspected the famous ironclad.

In dry dock for six weeks, the *Monitor* underwent an extensive overhaul of her engines and boilers. Other improvements were made, including a new iron shield installed around the top of the turret. The iron hull was scraped clean of barnacles and freshly painted so that she looked good as new. By November, the *Monitor* was ready to return to service.

In December 1862, after the *Monitor* had returned to Hampton Roads, word spread to the North that the Confederates were planning to use a new ironclad to break the blockade at Wilmington, North Carolina. "Send the *Monitor!*" went up the cry.

The crew received their new orders on Christmas Day, as they sat down to a lavish, three-hour dinner of soups, fish, and oysters that reportedly cost about $100 per man. The little *Monitor* started south from Hampton Roads on the afternoon of December 29. She went under tow, pulled by a paddle-wheel steamer, the *Rhode Island.* Soon after, the new ironclad USS *Montauk,* followed behind with her new captain, John Worden. The *Montauk* and another ironclad, the USS *Passaic*, were to join the *Monitor* in blockading Charleston, South Carolina, once the job was done in Wilmington. But, for the Monitor, it never came to that.

For the first day of the trip, all went well; the two vessels moved through a calm, glassy sea. On the morning of the second day, the water turned somewhat rough as the ships reached the open ocean. But it did not become dangerous until evening, when the wind rose to a gale. Still, jostled by the waves, the crew cheered as the *Monitor* prepared to round Cape Hatteras – the first ironclad to make that trip. So many ships had been wrecked and scattered by the cape's treacherous waters that it had become known as the "Graveyard of the Atlantic."

Forced below deck by the storm, the men joked about being free from the "monotonous inactive life." But the situation was serious. In what must have seemed like a recurring nightmare, water poured in the ship's hawse pipe, under the turret, and down the blower pipes. Captain Bankhead signaled the *Rhode Island* to stop, hoping to ride out the storm. The *Monitor*, coasting on the waves, rode no better, and the *Rhode Island* started up again.

The wind continued to increase almost to hurricane force. Captain Bankhead ordered the big power pump started. He became alarmed when the engineers reported that the water was still gaining. It had reached the ash pits of the fire boxes and was sloshing around the coal bunkers. He ordered a red lantern hoisted on the flagpole atop the turret, a prearranged distress signal. At the same time, he had the towing cable cut and let go his anchor to bring the *Monitor* head-on to the wind.

Waves thirty feet high were breaking over the ironclad, at times completely covering it so that the crew of the *Rhode Island* thought the *Monitor* had gone down. Captain Stephen Decatur Trenchard of the steamer launched two boats in the mad sea to aid the foundering vessel. As they were launched, the *Monitor's* towline, trailing from the *Rhode Island's* stern, became tangled in a paddle wheel. The *Rhode Island* drifted down on the helpless *Monitor,* narrowly missing a collision and crushing in the gunwale of one small boat caught between them.

The other boat reached the ironclad. Her deck was now under water, and the crew of the small boat pulled against the waves with their oars to keep the little craft from being washed aboard the sinking ship. A few men attempted the dangerous passage from the top of the turret to the rescue boat alongside. Some made it; others were washed away by the sweeping waves. When the rescue boat was full of drenched crewmen from the *Monitor,* Master's Mate Rodney Browne, who was the boat's commander, started back to the *Rhode Island*, which had now drifted half a mile away.

Aboard the *Monitor*, Captain Bankhead formed a bucket brigade to throw water out of the top of the turret. He had no hope of saving the ship by this puny effort, but it gave the men something to do and kept their minds off the great danger. Grenville Weeks, a surgeon on the *Monitor*, noted that "some sang as they worked, and . . . the voices, mingling with the roar of the waters, sounded like a defiance to the Ocean." Finally, Bankhead ordered: "It is madness to remain here any longer . . . let each man save himself." The captain returned to his cabin to retrieve his coat, took "one lingering look and . . . left the *Monitor*'s cabin forever."

Master's Mate Brown and his crew - all of whom later received the Medal of Honor for their night's work - returned to the stricken vessel for a second load. A seaman named Francis Butts, who was second-in-line in the bucket brigade, suddenly found that there was no one above him to take his bucket. From the top of the tower, he saw Brown's boat again pull up alongside. Captain Bankhead and Lieutenant Greene were on deck, clinging to a guide rope with two seamen. As he watched, the seamen were swept away. He fastened a safety line around his waist and climbed down from the turret. Twice, as he made his way across the deck, giant seas swept over him, and he dangled underwater at the end of his line like a fish on a hook. He finally reached the boat. As he looked back, he saw some men atop the turret, afraid to venture onto the deck below to reach the rescue craft.

In an account both tragic and comic, Butts described the danger and difficulty of getting aboard the *Rhode Island* itself. The waves lifted the rescue boat to the level of the steamer's rail, then dropped it far down to its keel. On the crest of a wave, Butts and an ensign grabbed a rope near the vessel's bow. The boat dropped out from beneath them, leaving them swinging in the air as the boat was swept toward the stern. With water-logged clothes, they could not climb aboard, and in the shrieking wind their cries for help could not be heard. The ensign weakened first and dropped off to his death in the sea. Finally, Butts could hang on no longer and followed him - just when the lifeboat was swept back under him. "Where did he come from?" a sailor on the lifeboat cried, as Butts tumbled aboard.

Paymaster William Keeler later recounted a similarly harrowing escape: "I divested myself of the greater portion of my clothing to afford me greater facilities for swimming . . . & attempted to descend the ladder leading down the outside of the turret, but found it full of men hesitating but desiring to make the perilous passage of the deck. . . . I found a rope hanging from one of the awning stanchions over my head & slid down it to the deck. A huge wave passed over me tearing me from my footing. . . . I was carried . . . ten or twelve yards from the vessel when . . . the wave threw me against the vessel's side near one of the iron stanchions which supported the life line;

this I grasped with all the energy of desperation & . . . was hauled into the boat."

One by one, the survivors managed to board the *Rhode Island*, and Brown started on a third rescue trip. As the lifeboat climbed the waves, he could see the red lantern on the *Monitor's* staff bobbing in the distance. Then, as he topped another wave, it was gone. The *Monitor* had plunged to the bottom of the sea ten miles east of Cape Hatteras in North Carolina. Sixteen men were lost in the rescue operation, or went down with the ship. Captain Bankhead had tried desperately to reach or coax the men out of the turret, but terrified by what they had seen of the rescue effort, they would not budge. One hundred and forty years later, in August 2002, the skeletal remains of two of the men were found still in the turret, recovered from the bottom of the Atlantic.

The famous ironclads were no more. "What the fire of the enemy failed to do, the elements have accomplished," Paymaster Keeler wrote to his wife. But there were others to take their places. Although no later battle achieved the fame of the *Monitor-Virginia* duel, the clang of shells on metal would sound again and again as new floating iron fortresses of both sides joined the long and bitter war.

6
"WITHOUT REGARD FOR MEN OR MONEY"

Where the Ohio River joins the Mississippi, the tip of Illinois points like a sword toward the south. This was the southernmost territory controlled by the Union. It drove deep into the Confederacy, separating the slave states of Kentucky and Missouri, which lie on opposite banks of the two rivers. From here, the mighty Mississippi meanders south in swinging loops for 1,100 miles to the Gulf of Mexico - 490 miles away as the crow flies.

The Mississippi and its tributaries were the highways of the West at the time of the Civil War. Good north-south roads were nonexistent, and there were few railroads. Northern control of these rivers would deprive the South of the beef and grain and the good fighting men of Arkansas, Texas, and most of Louisiana. To gain control of the rivers, the Union needed an inland navy.

A man named James Buchanan Eads built a fleet of ironclads, which would play a crucial role in gaining this control and winning the war in the West for the Union. When the war started, Eads was a retired millionaire living in St. Louis. He had made his money raising wrecks from the bottom of the Mississippi with a fleet of salvage vessels that he called submarines, but everybody else called snag boats. Eads had been inspired by his reading about Louis Napoleon's floating batteries. Five months before construction of the *Monitor* began, Eads was summoned to Washington with a plan to convert his biggest snag boat into an ironclad warship. Navy Secretary Welles liked the idea, but the Navy had nothing to say about the war on western waters - that was Army business. The Army was not interested in Eads's converted boat. Instead, it contracted with him to build seven new ironclads. Eads guaranteed to build the vessels in sixty-five days.

Eads was not an Ericsson. There was no inventive genius in the ships that he built. He did not even design them. They were planned by a naval architect named Samuel M. Pook and were generally called "Pook Turtles." But Eads was a man who could get things done. Within two weeks, 4,000 men were at work in forests, foundries, and shops in eight states. Telegraph wires to Cincinnati and Pittsburgh hummed with instructions for making twenty-one engines and thirty-five boilers. And since this was the North, where industries were flourishing, the order could be filled.

The first iron armor of the war was rolled in St. Louis and Louisville. Sawmills whined in Minnesota and Michigan, cutting timber for the turtles. After forty-five days, on October 12, 1861, the hull of the *St. Louis* was launched, soon to be followed by her sister ships *Carondelet, Cincinnati, Louisville, Mound City, Cairo,* and *Pittsburgh.*

The Eads-built ironclads were flat-bottomed scows 175 feet long and nearly fifty-two feet wide. A single paddle wheel was set into the stern. An oaken casemate with sloping sides two feet thick formed a box that encased the paddle wheel, engines, and guns. Each vessel mounted three powerful guns pointing forward, four lesser weapons in each broadside, and two light guns aimed aft.

Although the ships looked something like the *Virginia* in profile, they were much less powerful and were designed according to a different fighting concept. They were expected to fight head-on, so that only the front part of the casemate and the sides abreast of the boilers and engines had a special metal covering - iron plates no more than two and one-half inches thick. The stern and a large part of the sides were unarmored. Later, Eads converted his snag boat into an ironclad, bigger and stronger than the seven sister ships, and named her the *Benton*. He also armored a big river ferry, the *Essex*. These nine ships were the original inland ironclads.

By the time the ironclads were delivered at Cairo, Illinois, Brigadier General Ulysses S. Grant had arrived to take command. Three Confederate forts blocked his route south - one at Columbus, Kentucky, on the Mississippi; a second, Fort Henry, on the Tennessee River; and a third, Fort Donelson, on the Cumberland River, twelve miles east of Fort Henry. Grant decided that the works at Columbus were too strong to be attacked. But this position would be cut off if he could take the other two forts.

The campaign against forts Henry and Donelson was a joint Army and Navy operation. Flag Officer Andrew Foote, in charge of the river fleet, led off with the *Essex, Carondelet, Cincinnati,* and *St. Louis* - he did not have enough sailors to man the other ironclads. General Grant followed with as much of his army as he could crowd aboard available river steamers. The convoy started from Cairo, steamed forty miles up the Ohio to the mouth of the Tennessee, then another fifty miles up that river to anchor below Fort Henry. There the soldiers disembarked, and promptly bogged down in the flooded swamps that bordered the river.

Fort Henry was an earthwork lying low on the riverbank. It mounted twelve guns pointing downstream and was manned by 4,000 raw recruits. The black smoke of the Union armada indicated an overpowering force, and Confederate General Lloyd Tilghman, commander of the garrison, prudently decided to send most of his men overland to Fort Donelson, keeping only fifty-four gunners to fight a delaying action.

While the Union army floundered in the mud, the ironclads steamed forward four abreast to attack. The *Cincinnati* opened the fight from a mile away, her shots falling short of Fort Henry's poorly designed riverside embankment. The *Essex*, her guns elevated higher, started to raise showers of dirt from the earthen parapets as her gunners found the range. The ships slowly advanced to within 500 yards of the fort where they "stood on their wheels" - using only enough power to hold them steady in the swift current.

For almost an hour, the noisy, smoky cannonade continued. The *Carondelet* was hit thirty times, the *St. Louis* seven, the *Cincinnati* thirty-two. The shells cracked the iron plates but did not come through. Then the *Essex* swung sideways with the current, and a heavy shell pierced the unarmored casemate and entered the middle boiler, filling the forward part of the ship with steam and boiling water. Both pilots were scalded to death. The helmsman was found dead, one hand on the wheel and the other on the signal cord. The badly burned captain and most of the men on the forward gun deck dived through ports into the water. The *Essex*, out of control, drifted slowly down the river, clouds of steam swirling from her ports.

At this point, the battle turned against the Confederates. Their biggest gun exploded, and another was filled with earth by a shell that burst below it. A shifting wind blew the battle smoke toward them, making their targets invisible. Two guns were hit squarely on the muzzles at almost the same instant, and both crews were felled by flying fragments. The ironclads moved closer to the fort. Only four Confederate guns were in action when General Tilghman surrendered his devastated fort. Grant arrived to find the Confederate commander aboard the *Cincinnati* having a friendly drink with Flag Officer Foote. In their first battle, the inland ironclads had conquered a fort without help from the army.

Grant got his troops out of the swamp and started overland on the road to Fort Donelson. Foote went back to Cairo to replace the battered *Essex* and *Cincinnati* with the *Louisville* and the *Pittsburgh*. These new ships joined the *St. Louis* and the *Carondelet*, and the four steamed up the Cumberland River toward Donelson. As Grant threw his army around the fort and mounted artillery to bombard it from the landward side, the ironclads advanced to what they believed would be their second victory.

But Donelson was a different story from Henry. Its three batteries, mounting fifteen guns, were well placed on a bluff above the river, harder targets than the water-level guns of Fort Henry. Their plunging fire hit the sloping, slightly armored casemates of the ironclads at right angles. A solid 128-pound shot came through the forward casemate of the *Carondelet*, glanced off a temporary barricade of coal bags around the boilers, and then bounced around the engine room. In the words of one engineer, "it seemed to bound after the men like a wild beast pursuing its prey."

As well as being up against a stronger fort, the Union steamers were hindered by a faulty battle plan. Emboldened by their success at Fort Henry, they moved in closer, trying to overpower the Confederate batteries. The fort's cannons were lighter than Foote realized; if he had stayed farther out in the river and used his heavier guns to good effect, his ships would not have been damaged so severely. As it was, the wheel ropes of the *St. Louis* and the *Louisville* were soon shot away, and both vessels drifted downstream out of control. The *Pittsburgh* followed, leaking badly. The *Carondelet* bravely carried on the fight alone but could not long withstand the concentrated fire of the fort.

Her stack, pilothouse, anchor, and boat cranes were shot away. Then one of the bow guns exploded, setting the ship on fire. Finally, two shots entered the bow ports and instantly killed four men.

The *Carondelet* started to fall back, still keeping her head toward the fort and firing her remaining bow guns. The gun captains watched for approaching shells and shouted "Look out, down!" to their crews. Most of those who hit the deck were spared as shells entered the ports, but some of the younger men, from excitement or bravado, failed to obey. One shell came through a port and struck down two more members of the gun crew.

The ironclads returned to Cairo for repairs, leaving Grant to capture Donelson. With its fall and that of Fort Henry, the Confederates found Columbus's Mississippi River position indefensible and evacuated the town. Grant pursued, starting south on the first march of his road to fame - a succession of victories in which the ironclads played an important and effective role.

The next Confederate stronghold downriver was Island No. 10, so called because it was the tenth island on the Mississippi south of the Ohio River's intersection. This long island was well armed with more than fifty big guns and a floating battery mounting sixteen more. Six of the ironclads headed cautiously down the Mississippi. Foote had learned that his armor was not shellproof at close range;

the thin plating at the bow and total lack of steel at the sides and stern were grave handicaps. Also, this time the weakly powered ships were upstream from the fort. A disabled ship would float into it instead of away from it. For three weeks, Foote shelled the Confederate works from a distance of 2,000 yards without effect. One Union colonel said, contemptuously, that the Navy was "shelling the state of Tennessee at long range."

Meanwhile, Union General John Pope had bypassed the island. He had cut a canal through a neck of land out of reach for Southern guns and floated his men through on barges. He was downstream from the Confederate defenses, but on the wrong side of the river - at New Madrid. He could not cross until batteries on the opposite bank were silenced. He asked Foote for an ironclad to do the job.

It seemed like a suicide mission. The ironclad would have to steam downriver past the guns of Island No. 10, for Pope's canal was too shallow to be navigated. In passing the island, the ship would expose its unarmored side to every Confederate gun at point-blank range. Only one of Foote's officers thought that a ship could make it through. Captain Henry A. Walke volunteered to try with the *Carondelet,* and Foote reluctantly agreed to let him make the attempt. To protect the *Carondelet's* exposed side, a barge loaded high with bales of hay and bags of coal was lashed alongside. Captain

Walke remarked that she looked like a farmer's wagon heading for market.

The run was made on what should have been a dark night, but a violent storm broke, adding sheets of rain and crashes of thunder to the excitement - and flashes of lightning to reveal the ship to Confederate gunners. The ship got past the first two batteries without detection. Then the dry soot in her stack caught fire, and a pencil of flame shot up into the wild night. A lightning flash disclosed the source of the flame to the Southerners, and they ran to their guns. The muzzles of the guns had been depressed to keep the rain out. Aboard the *Carondelet*, Walke was elated to hear the Confederate officers shouting "Elevate, elevate!" They had miscalculated the range; the ironclad was so close under the Southern guns that, had they been fired in their depressed position, she might have been blown out of the water.

At 2:00 a.m., the *Carondelet* safely reached Pope's headquarters at New Madrid. The *Pittsburgh* joined her the following night, and the two ships quickly silenced the Confederate batteries. Assisted by Pope's boats that had gone through the canal, they escorted Pope's men across. The outflanked Confederates tried to retreat. Those that remained on Island No. 10 surrendered to Flag Officer Foote. The inland ironclads had taken another long and important step down the river.

So far, the ironclads had met no opposition from other ships. The first encounter came as a surprise, on a Sunday morning in May 1862. The river war had moved down to Fort Pillow, on a bluff upriver from Memphis, Tennessee. Too strong to be taken from the river, Fort Pillow was an objective that the Navy could not attempt without Army help. While the Navy waited, it annoyed the Southerners by mooring a mortar boat behind a bend in the river to lob a shell into the fort every half hour. One ironclad stood guard over the mortar boat while the rest of the fleet anchored upstream. On May 10, the *Cincinnati* had this duty. Her crew was scrubbing down the ship on this misty morning when a strange fleet came steaming up the river.

The Confederates had converted river tugs into iron-beaked rams. Although nearly defenseless - they carried only one or two guns - these fast, powerful little steamers could be deadly against the unarmored sterns and sides of the ironclads, which they could easily outrun and outmaneuver. Eight of these rams had dashed out from under the guns of Fort Pillow to make an attack on the Northern ship.

The ironclad slipped her cables and stood out into the river. She had time for only one broadside before the leading ram crashed into her side, opening a hole six by twelve feet. A second broadside sent the ram reeling down the river, but not before another ram had swung around to crash into the

Cincinnati's unprotected stern, and a third into her side. The ironclad went down.

The rest of the armored fleet could not see the action through the mist, but when they heard the guns, they left their moorings. In rather ragged order, they started downriver. The *Mound City* arrived first, collided head-on with a Confederate ram, turned into the bank, and sank. The *Benton* and *Carondelet* came next. When the latter put a shot through the boiler of a ram, the Confederate fleet turned tail and took refuge under the guns of Fort Pillow. Although the two sunken ships were raised and repaired, it was a costly morning for the Union ironclads.

The Southerners appeared to have won the day, but the following month they were forced by low rations and lower morale to withdraw from Fort Pillow. The rams moved downriver to Memphis, followed soon after by the Union fleet, which anchored north of the city. This fleet was very shortly reinforced by seven fast, ram-equipped craft - of which the Southerners knew nothing.

When the eight agile Confederate rams next advanced upriver, they expected to meet only five lumbering ironclads. But, as the people of the area crowded the river bluffs to watch what they believed would be a Southern victory, two Unions rams suddenly dashed through the slowly moving line of armored ships. The Union ram *Queen of the*

West crashed into the Confederate *Colonel Lovell* and cut her in half. The Confederates' *Beauregard* and *Price* made for the Union ram *Monarch* and missed, then crashed into each other. The *Price* crawled to the bank and sank. The *Monarch* swung around and rammed the *Beauregard* at the same time that the *Benton* put a shot in the Southerner's boiler and blew her up. During the entire engagement, the guns of the Union ironclads had been hammering away at anything flying the Stars and Bars. They sank two rams and captured two others. Only one Confederate ship escaped down the river. Later that day, Memphis surrendered to the fleet. The river was now open to the half-way point - the fortress city of Vicksburg.

More Ironclads for the Confederacy

While the ironclads were opening the northern Mississippi, Admiral David Glasgow Farragut was assembling a Union fleet in the Gulf of Mexico to move up the river. It was a powerful force of eight big ships, nine gunboats, and a fleet of mortar schooners - but it had no ironclads.

Ninety miles up the Mississippi, at New Orleans, the Confederates had finished one ironclad and had two others under construction. The latter were of the *Virginia* type, but bigger and stronger than the *Virginia* - or they would be if they could be finished. The *Louisiana* was already armed and armored, but the engines, which had been taken from a river steamer, would not work. They never did. The *Mississippi,* at the time of Farragut's attack, was armored only up to her gun deck. She had engines - but the main propeller shaft was slowly being turned out on a lathe in faraway Richmond. Southern industry - or rather the lack of it - was again proving to be a fatal bottleneck in the Confederate war effort.

The one finished ironclad at New Orleans was the little *Manassas.* Originally she had been a powerful tugboat. Private citizens had tried to convert her into an ironclad privateer by building up a rounded hood of twelve-inch oak topped with one and one-half inches of iron plate. She looked exactly like half an egg floating narrow end forward, with one large gun and a smokestack sticking out of the top. After the armor was added, her speed was only four miles an hour. Too slow for a privateer, she was taken into the Confederate Navy.

The *Manassas* had already proved her worth long before Farragut's fleet arrived. Actually, she was the first American ironclad to have seen action. In October 1861 - five months before the *Virginia* sailed from Norfolk - she had led an attack on four Union vessels that were blockading at Head of the Passes, a point about fifteen miles from the Gulf, where several branches of the Mississippi Delta join. She had come downstream followed by three fire rafts chained together and, behind these, five wooden gunboats.

The plan was that the *Manassas* would sneak up, ram one of the Union ships, and send up a rocket. This was the signal to ignite and cast off the fire rafts, which would float down on the wooden blockade vessels. But the plan went totally awry. The *Manassas* missed her target, the rafts grounded upstream, and the gunboats fired ineffectively from afar. No one was hurt, although the Union Navy's pride was severely injured by the encounter. In the confusion, one Union ship was temporarily abandoned, and the next day, all four retreated cautiously to the Gulf.

Farragut, however, was not deterred by the reputation of the *Manassas,* nor was he much concerned about the Confederate naval force that stood between him and New Orleans; he was resolved to carry out his orders to steam up to New Orleans from the Gulf. The dozen converted steamboats and tugs that made up the Southern Navy were no match for any of his big ships, and he probably knew, from spies, that the ironclad *Louisiana* was a powerless floating battery. At 2:00 a.m. on April 24, 1862, Farragut started up the river. The dangerous part of the attack, passing the two forts below the city, was accomplished with much smoke and noise, blazing fire rafts, flaming guns - and little damage.

The *Louisiana*, moored near the forts, was not very effective. She was invulnerable but also immobile.

Union shells clanged harmlessly against her sides of iron. A nine-inch shell from the *Louisiana* buried itself in the bow of the sloop of war *Brooklyn*, but failed to explode. The ironclad's guns also cut up the sloop *Iroquois*, but the rest of the fleet got past safely.

And then the spunky *Manassas* attacked - pitting her puny ram and single gun against the entire Union fleet. She first tried to ram the big *Pensacola,* but the sloop avoided the Southerner's clumsy rush and peppered it with a broadside. Then the little, armored tug ran down the line of ships, firing her gun when it would bear and seeking a chance to ram. The *Manassas* caught the *Brooklyn* unaware and slammed into her side, but the tug's light weight and slow speed could do little harm to the giant. The skipper of the *Brooklyn later* told how he looked down from the deck at the pygmy far below pressing its nose against his ship's side. While he was watching, a man crawled out of the hatch at the *Manassas*'s stern and ran forward to inspect the damage. Suddenly he tumbled into the water. The captain of the *Brooklyn* called his leadsman, "Did you see that man fall?" "Yes, sir," replied the sailor, "I helped him. I hit him in the head with my hand lead."

The *Manassas* started back up the river, again running the gauntlet of fire from the big wooden ships. In the light of blazing fire rafts and burning Confederate gunboats, Farragut spied her and signaled for the *Mississippi* to ram. (There was a

Mississippi on both sides.) The big side-wheeler swung out of line and bore down on the tiny tug. The *Manassas* was now on fire, her light armor a shell-pierced sieve. Lieutenant A. F. Warley, the Southern skipper who had fought so bravely with his ship, turned her nose into the bank and ordered his crew to take to the woods. The *Mississippi* fired two broadsides into the gallant little vessel. She drifted away from the bank and floated downstream, burning until she exploded.

Before the Confederates surrendered New Orleans, they burned their unfinished *Mississippi*. While the surrender of the downriver forts was being negotiated aboard the Union revenue cutter *Harriet Lane*, the captain of the still unharmed *Louisiana* set his ship afire and cast her loose. She drifted toward the cutter and exploded, almost swamping the *Harriet Lane* and the surrender conference. The Southern Navy at New Orleans was wiped out. Farragut steamed up the river to meet the ironclads at Vicksburg, the last Confederate stronghold on the river.

A lesser man than Confederate Lieutenant Isaac Newton Brown would have been dismayed at the first sight of his new command. As he stood on the edge of the flooded Yazoo River, the *Arkansas*, moored to the riverbank four miles away, looked more like a large chicken coop than an ironclad. Before Memphis fell, the Southerners had towed the unfinished ship down the Mississippi and far up the Yazoo out of harm's way. Brown's orders were to finish her "without regard for men or money." The orders, however, did not say where he could get the men, money, or materials.

When he arrived to take charge on April 28, 1862, the ship's armor was in place only about a foot above the water line. Brown was told that the remaining iron - in the form of railroad rails - was at the bottom of the river on a sunken barge. If he needed more metal, he would have to pull up track from deserted spur lines in the interior. The rails were interlocked to form a three-inch layer over the *Arkansas*'s one-foot-thick oaken casemate, which had been lined with compressed cotton bales for further protection.

The *Arkansas* had ten guns: two in the bow, two in the stern, and three in each broadside. Her sharp prow carried an iron beak for a ram. Each of her two engines, homemade in Memphis, drove a separate screw propeller. Unfortunately, though, when one engine stopped - as it quite frequently did - the remaining propeller would spin the ship in circles, regardless of the rudder.

Despite this dismal picture, Brown went to work immediately. He fished up the sunken barge, put the iron on the deck, and steamed down to Yazoo City. Here he was closer to the menacing Union fleet, but he felt that getting more workers was worth the risk. He borrowed forges and slave blacksmiths from neighboring plantations. He sent wagons out to collect more railroad rails. When everything was in place, the finished ship was a rusty red, but since Brown had no paint, she stayed that way.

The falling water level on the Yazoo made it necessary for the *Arkansas* to head for the Mississippi at once. So, on July 13, Brown started down the Yazoo, intending to aid the Confederate forces at New Orleans.

He realized, however, that first he would have to reckon with a large Union fleet - Farragut's ships up from the Gulf plus several rams and the Eads ironclads - which was anchored on the Mississippi between the mouth of the Yazoo and Vicksburg. The Yankees themselves knew an ironclad was being built somewhere on the Yazoo, and just as the *Arkansas* was steaming down the river, they decided to send the ironclad *Carondelet,* the ram *Queen of the West,* and the gunboat *Tyler* up to investigate.

On the morning of July 15, the three Union ships met the Southern ironclad about seven miles up the Yazoo. The *Arkansas* routed the ram and the gallant *Carondelet* easily, although in the process, her smokestack was perforated by their gunners. Then she followed the fleeing *Tyler* into the Mississippi where the rest of the Union fleet of more than thirty large warships, ironclads, and rams rode at anchor.

As the forest of Federal masts and smokestacks came into Brown's view, he cursed the shell holes in his ship's stack that cut her speed to little more than one mile an hour, much too slow for ramming. The larger Union ships were anchored in line with the rams behind them. Brown ordered his helmsman to run close along the line so that the rams could not get up enough speed to hurt the *Arkansas*. He depressed his broadside guns and fired at the water line of each ship as he passed, receiving a full broadside from each vessel in return.

Although twenty-seven of her crew were laid low when two Union shells crashed through her casemate, the *Arkansas* made it past the fleet to the safety of Vicksburg. There the dead and wounded were sent ashore. Some soldiers from a Missouri regiment, who had volunteered only as far as Vicksburg, also left. And Brown, with only half a crew, started making repairs.

Irate at being caught napping, Farragut had no intention of letting the Southern ship get away with shaming the U.S. Navy. He was all for charging down and attacking the ram under the shore batteries immediately, but it was evening before his unprepared fleet could get ready to move. Brown had anticipated such an attack and had moved his vessel to a new mooring beside a red clay bank. Against this, the rust-colored ship was almost invisible in the dusk. When Farragut's fleet finally attacked, each of the big Union ships fired a broadside at the *Arkansas* as it passed. Only one eleven-inch shell hit her, but it came through the armor and further reduced the remnants of the ship's crew.

For a week, the Northerners let the plucky Southern ship alone. The *Essex*, which had taken such a beating at Fort Henry, returned from upstream newly repaired and with a fresh crew. At sunrise on July 22, the Union ironclad and the *Queen of the West* braved the fire of the shore batteries and attacked the *Arkansas.*

Brown had barely enough men left to man the two forward guns. One of the engines was disabled as well. He cast off his forward line so that the ram-armed bow drifted out to face the enemy. The *Essex* swerved to avoid it as the ships exchanged shots. One shell penetrated the *Arkansas,* split one of her guns, and killed half her already depleted crew. The remaining Confederates raced to their broadside guns as the *Essex* ran alongside them. Then, with the two ships facing each other muzzle to muzzle, they fired into the Yankee vessel. A lucky shot hit the *Essex's* engines and forced the disabled ironclad to float helplessly downstream. But the harried Southerners had no time to rest before the oncoming *Queen* rammed them. The blow was little more than a nudge, and as the *Queen* backed off, the *Arkansas's* gunners fired a broadside at her that sent her limping out of battle. There were only fourteen Confederates left by then, but they and their rusty ship seemed tireless.

The days following the battle were quiet. As the ship was being repaired, and a new crew assembled, Brown went to bed ashore with a fever from the wound received in the Yazoo duel the previous week. He warned his superiors that under no condition should the limping ship be moved. However, his advice was ignored, and the *Arkansas* was ordered into action under the command of Lieutenant Henry Stevens. He was to move the ship downstream to support a Confederate attack on Baton Rouge. Several times during the trip, the engines gave out. One breakdown was so serious that the engineers had to set up a forge on the gun deck and labor all night to repair the engines. When they set out again in the morning, the *Essex* was seen coming upstream. But the *Arkansas's* port engine stopped, and the ship circled into the bank in a position from which her guns could not fire on the approaching *Essex*.

In order to prevent her capture, Stevens, with tears streaming down his face, ordered the crew ashore and remained aboard alone to set fire to the ship. Because he waited so long to make sure that the fires had caught, he had to dive overboard and swim to safety. "With colors flying," Brown later wrote, "the gallant *Arkansas*, whose decks had never been pressed by the foot of an enemy, was blown into the air."

The Iron Dummy

Vicksburg remained the focal point of the Union attack on the Confederacy. And, thinking the Southern river fleet demolished, Washington had high hopes that Farragut's fleet and the river ironclads along with a few troops could take the city quickly. This was wishful thinking. On a long line of bluffs, the big guns of the fortress city completely dominated the river up, down, and across. Most of them proved too high for the ships' cannons to reach. So Farragut went back to the Gulf, the river ironclads stayed above Vicksburg, and the Confederates remained in control of the center section of the river. However, this stalemate was broken temporarily by a fake Union ironclad.

The story of this ironic interlude in the ironclad river war begins in February 1863, when a new Union ironclad, the *Indianola,* was sent down the Mississippi to guard the mouth of the Red River, below Vicksburg. Her job was to contain some Southern ships known to be up the river. But in short order, two Southern rams swept down on her and sank her. David Dixon Porter, who had by this time been named commander of the Union river fleet, said it was "the most humiliating affair that has occurred during this rebellion." Particularly galling was the fact that he could not spare another ironclad to go after the rams - General Grant had arrived above the city and had plans for them. Porter was supposed to be given several powerful, double-turret ironclad monitors. But they were far from ready. Porter decided to try to chase the rams away with a dummy double-turreted monitor.

An old barge was discovered and served as the base for the dummy. Two large hogsheads, with wooden guns, were set on top for turrets; two beef barrels full of tar were the stacks. Dummy small boats and a pilothouse completed the "ironclad." The tar was lit, and the fierce-looking, black-painted barge was set adrift on the river above the city of Vicksburg.

Every gun on the bluffs blasted at the dummy, but apparently had little result. The telegraph lines to the South crackled with the news that the North had a vessel so strong it was proof against the heaviest cannons. Meanwhile, a group of Confederates downstream heard of the ironclad's approach as they struggled feverishly to raise the sunken *Indianola*. Fearing her recapture by the monster, they totally destroyed the damaged vessel - all because, the Southerners sadly realized later, of a wooden barge belching black tar smoke. The Northerners, on the other hand, were so elated by their dummy's success that they quickly built another, which also enjoyed an effective reign of terror.

At about the same time, Porter embarked on an expedition that resulted in an equally bizarre chapter in ironclad history. Grant's first plan for taking Vicksburg was a combined attack by his forces from the East, and William Tecumseh Sherman's from the North. To help destroy the city's defenses, Grant sought naval support by Porter from the upper Yazoo River, which flows behind the city, almost parallel to the Mississippi. The lower Yazoo proved too shallow for the ironclads to travel through. Porter's next attempt was to try to reach the upper river by navigating through a series of bayous - virgin forests flooded by spring rains. He set out with five ironclads, four mortars, and four tugs.

The water in the bayous was fifteen feet deep, but it swirled around trees from which raccoons, wildcats, and snakes, seeking safety from the floods, peered down on the invaders. The *Cincinnati*, in the lead, found that it could clear a channel by backing off and butting a big tree out of the way. But the overhanging branches caved in pilothouses, knocked down stacks, and tore off lifeboats. The way was so confused that, at times, the various vessels pointed in four different directions.

For four days, they inched forward. Then they came to a pleasant pond covered with patches of green. The tug in the lead suddenly stopped amidst the verdure. The *Cincinnati* went forward to help and she, too, became immobile. The green patches were willows growing from the bottom, and the branches wound themselves around the paddle wheels, making the pond a deadly trap.

While the *Cincinnati* was held fast, shells started to drop around her from an invisible battery of Confederate field artillery. Porter landed howitzers and drove the Southerners off, but they quickly took a new position and renewed their fire. In the meantime, two of the ironclads passed hawsers to the *Cincinnati* and hauled her back out of the willows.

A slave then warned them that two regiments were hastening to box in the ironclads from the rear. At this point, there was nothing they could do except turn back.

No sooner had the fleet managed to escape to the broad waters of the Mississippi than they became involved in a new - and ultimately successful - plan for the capture of Vicksburg. First, the ships had to run past the thundering guns of the fort. Then they provided covering fire for Grant's march down the opposite bank of the Mississippi and across it to attack the city from the south.

In the final phase of the siege, the main role of the armored ships was to cut off the Confederate escape route across the river. One of the ships, the *Cincinnati*, was lost on a reconnaissance cruise. But the others were still in action when, on July 4, 1863, the city finally surrendered. The Mississippi was firmly in Union hands from Cairo, Illinois, to the Gulf of Mexico.

7

"THE CROWNING ACT OF THIS WAR"

Fort Sumter, in the harbor of Charleston, South Carolina, was a symbol. The attack upon it and its capture by the Confederates started the fighting between the North and South. The Northern press and public - and the president - wanted it back. After Farragut sailed past the forts in the lower Mississippi and captured New Orleans, and after Porter ran past the Vicksburg batteries to help General Grant take that city, many Northerners felt that Sumter, followed by Charleston itself, could be taken in a naval siege. There were nine Union ironclads anchored off Morris Island just outside the Charleston harbor. If Farragut could defy two forts with wooden ships, it should be a simple matter to conquer one fort with those wonderful ironclads - or so the Northern public thought.

Actually, Charleston was a far more formidable objective than New Orleans. Fort Sumter stood on one side of the channel that led into the harbor, and Fort Moultrie, on Sullivan's Island, commanded the other. There were numerous smaller batteries on points and islands in the outer harbor. In the spring of 1863, when the North planned an all-out attack against the Southern citadel, more firepower could be concentrated on the channel than at any other spot on the continent.

The Confederates, moreover, had obstructed the channel with wooden piles, a floating log boom, a cable with trailing ropes to snag propellers, and mines (then called torpedoes). Nevertheless, the Northern press and public clamored for the attack. At the highest echelons of the United States Navy, there was the sense that this battle, if successful, would decide the war. About Charleston, Secretary of the Navy Gideon Welles wrote in his diary: "There is no city so culpable, or against which there is so much animosity." Inevitably, Rear Admiral Samuel Du Pont, the crusty commander of the fleet off Charleston harbor, was ordered to make the attack. Assistant Secretary of the Navy Gustavus Fox wrote to Du Pont: "The crowning act of this war out to be by the navy. . . . I pray you give us Charleston if possible . . . for the Fall of Charleston is the fall of Satan's Kingdom."

Of the nine ironclads in his fleet, seven were monitors, similar to the original *Monitor* except that their pilothouses were on top of the turrets. The other two ironclads were the *New Ironsides* and the *Keokuk*, an experimental ship. The *New Ironsides,* one of the earliest ironclads built by the North, was the strongest ship in the Union Navy. She was 250 feet long and mounted eight large guns in each broadside. Her three-inch armor plating extended well below the water line as well as for three feet above it. But the ship did have some faults. Incredibly, her pilothouse was placed behind the stack and no one could see directly forward. When the stack was cut down so that the captain and pilot could see over it, they were almost smothered by smoke, cinders, and fumes. Also, the ship could not be steered very well at slow speeds or in shoal water.

In view of the ironclads' limitations and the harbor's defenses, Admiral Du Pont doubted that the armored ships could take Charleston. But in response to the president's urging, he reluctantly ordered his fleet into the harbor on the night of April 7, 1863. The monitor *Weehawken* led the fleet into battle - pushing a huge raft with grapnels trailing from the forward end which were supposed to snag and explode underwater mines. The raft brought only trouble from the start. More than once it came down on the *Weehawken*'s deck, and it also got under her bow and acted like a battering ram. The *Weehawken* finally cast it adrift.

It was two hours before the ships came within range of Moultrie and Sumter. The forts' gunners held their fire as the vessels slowly advanced. Suddenly, a torpedo exploded near the *Weehawken's* bow, lifting her in the water, but doing little damage. As the *Weehawken* crept forward again, she opened the battle with a shot from her fifteen-inch gun. It passed neatly through the Confederate flag that was flying on top of Fort Sumter.

When the *Weehawken* reached a buoy marking a turn in the channel, all the guns of the two major forts and the smaller batteries opened on her. The guns had been trained on this buoy and were waiting for the first ship to reach it. The *Weehawken* almost disappeared among the bursting shells and spouts of water. But the shot rang off her turret as she forged ahead, answering the fire from the forts as fast as her guns could be loaded. The second monitor came within range, and the third and fourth. When the *Weehawken* reached the first line of obstructions in the channel, her skipper decided that he could not get through and turned back. The ships that were following tried to turn after her, but instead the entire first division of the fleet fell into confusion.

The *New Ironsides*, fifth in line, had become unmanageable once she hit the slack shoal water a mile from the fort. Her pilot, fearing she would run aground, ordered the anchor let go. The two monitors behind bumped into her. When the anchor was raised, she drifted back, then anchored again. On shore, some Confederate engineers were jubilant. The flagship was sitting directly over a torpedo, made from a water boiler filled with hundreds of pounds of gunpowder. They pushed down the plunger that was supposed to send an electric current to fire the torpedo. Nothing happened. In laying the wire to the mine, the cable ship had drifted so far that the wire lay along the bottom in a mile-long arc. The loss of voltage was so great that an insufficient amount of current reached the mine to explode it.

Du Pont made a signal to ignore the actions of the *New Ironsides*, and the second division - three monitors and the *Keokuk* - steamed past her and into the battle. But unlike the battles of New Orleans or Vicksburg, the ships could not simply run past the batteries; they were forced to stay in the narrow confines of the harbor and exchange fire with the forts.

Now the entire fleet was engaged, with eight ships close to the forts and the *New Ironsides* at long range. The *Keokuk*, seemingly under better control than the monitors, forged ahead to within 600 yards of Sumter. However, in twenty minutes, she had been hit ninety times, and many shells penetrated her thin armor below the water line. She withdrew from battle and sank the next morning.

The other ironclads took a terrible beating, too, but they stood up under it. However, their firepower, which did little damage to the brick and concrete masonry of Fort Sumter, was slowly but severely reduced. The turrets became jammed on the *Passaic,* the *Nantucket,* and the *Nahant,* and a gun was disabled on the *Patapsco.* With the *Keokuk* out of battle, and the *New Ironsides* too far away to be effective, the fleet had only seven guns left to answer the blazing batteries of the forts. At the end of two hours, Du Pont signaled the fleet to break off the ineffective bombardment and retire.

During the battle, the forts fired 2,209 times, compared to only 139 shots from the fleet. The Union ships were hit 439 times, but Fort Sumter was struck squarely only fifty-five times. The amazing part of the battle, and final proof of the protection provided by iron armor, was that only one Union man was killed under the rain of Confederate fire. The helmsman of the *Nahant* had been felled by a flying bolt head. On the Southern side four men died - a flagpole fell on one, and a bursting Confederate gun accounted for the other three.

For almost two years, the Navy continued to menace the Charleston harbor, supporting the Army in repeated landing operations that gained footholds on the outlying islands. But the ironclads were not successful in subduing the city of Charleston - which did not fall until General

Sherman marched up the coast from Savannah and captured it from the landward side.

A bright spot for the Union in this long siege was the fact that the *New Ironsides* survived 250 hits, more than any ship in the history of the Navy had suffered. Scratched and dented, she came through unvanquished.

The *New Ironsides* had faced more than cannons, too; the Confederates had made a desperate attempt to sink the vessel with what then passed for a submarine. This was a freak craft called the *David*, a cigar-shaped vessel about fifty feet long and from five and a half to six feet wide. It ran nearly awash except for a one-man hatch from which it was steered, and a short stack in the middle of its back. It carried from four to six men and had a sixty-pound explosive charge attached to a long spar extending from its bow. On the dark night of October 5, 1863, Lieutenant W. T. Gassell, with three volunteers, took the *David* out of Charleston harbor to attack the *New Ironsides*.

The anchored Union blockaders were totally unprepared: They had no picket boats out and had not kept their calcium lights (Civil War searchlights) playing on the water to spot attackers. Aboard the flagship, a few sentinels walked the deck, the duty watch was asleep by the guns, and some officers were smoking and fishing from the stern. The officer of the deck, a young acting ensign named C. W. Howard, suddenly saw something floating toward the ship. He hailed, "Boat ahoy!" and got no answer. He hailed again. This time he was answered by a shotgun blast from the hatch of the *David* that mortally wounded him. As the crew was roused by the shot, a tremendous explosion shook the ship, and a column of water rose high in the air. The submarine's torpedo had crashed against the *New Ironsides's* armor under water. At the time, she appeared unharmed, but later inspections showed that a number of weakened plates had started to leak.

The wave caused by the blast swept back over the *David*, pouring down the hatch and stack, putting out the fire. Thinking that the vessel was sinking, Gassell ordered the crew over the side to swim to safety. He and two others left. The pilot, who could not swim, clung to the boat. After swimming a short time, the fireman noticed that the *David*'s hatch was still above water. He swam back, pulled the pilot aboard, started the fire, and took the submarine back to Charleston. Gassell and the remaining volunteer were found, exhausted, clinging to the anchor chain of a Union vessel and captured - a humiliating conclusion to their daring, but unsuccessful, attack.

Although the Confederacy was battered and besieged, the Southerners held off a major assault at Charleston. They were nearly as successful on another distant front of the war - in Texas. For while the salt-water ironclads of the Union Navy were trying to help one part of the Army capture Charleston, the inland ironclads set out to help another Union force invade Texas. A previous attempt from the Gulf had failed. Now it was planned that the Army would go up the Red River Valley to attack the Texas interior from the northeast corner of the state. The ironclads were to support them as far as Shreveport.

This route was possible only in the springtime, when the river was at flood height. So in March 1864, the fleet assembled on the Mississippi at the mouth of the Red River. Among the fifteen ironclads were most of the original Eads vessels, plus some new ones, including three river monitors and the *Eastport,* a ram captured from the Confederates.

The vessels proceeded without incident up the river to Grand Ecore, where they were to meet the Army. Admiral Porter, who was in command of the fleet, left most of it there and took the ironclad *Eastport* and some lighter-draft vessels up ahead to reconnoiter.

The heavy *Eastport* inched its way up the twisting river, occasionally touching bottom. It got as far as Springfield Landing, where it found the river blocked by a sunken steamer that stretched from bank to bank. While Porter was trying to find a way to remove the obstruction, a message came from the

Army commander. He had been defeated and was falling back, leaving Porter stranded deep in enemy territory. And the river, which should have been rising, was starting to fall; the springtime flood was, it was later learned, the lowest in twenty years.

The *Eastport* started back down the river, shepherding several smaller vessels before her. At one point, they were attacked from the bank by some 2,000 Confederate infantry, armed only with light field pieces. The *Eastport* returned the fire until the daring Confederates were forced to withdraw, leaving 700 dead. She continued downstream but kept running aground. When she grounded hopelessly amid snags and sunken logs, eight barrels of gunpowder were placed under each end of her casemate, and she was blown to pieces in the shallow river.

Meanwhile, the main body of the fleet was retreating down the Red River toward the Mississippi. Nine of the ironclads were trapped at Alexandria, to which the Army had retreated. Below them lay the Falls of Alexandria - two sets of rapids about a mile apart. The channel between the rapids was filled with rugged rocks around which the falling river swirled. There was only three feet of water in the falls, and the big ironclads needed seven. Deep in Confederate country, the situation of the ironclads seemed hopeless until a daring solution was suggested by Lieutenant Colonel Joseph Bailey of the Army Engineers.

Colonel Bailey had been a lumberman in Wisconsin before the war. He had often floated logs down shallow rivers by building dams to back up the water, then breaking the dams in the middle to let the timber shoot through. If this technique worked with logs, it might also succeed with ironclads. The naval officers did not have much confidence in this way of making a deep channel, but at this point, any idea was worth trying.

Many soldiers were put to work as woodsmen, and soon a network of fallen trees had begun to dam one side of the river. There were no trees on the other bank, but there were plenty of rocks and a few brick buildings. Bailey built some cribs, stretching out from the bank, and set the remaining troops to hauling rocks and tearing down buildings to fill them. As the two sides of the dam approached each other, four barges loaded with stones were sunk in the gap to close the dam.

In eight days, the work was completed, and the water started to back up behind the dam. It was almost deep enough to float the ironclads downstream when the pressure suddenly carried away two barges in the dam and the pent-up water started to sweep through. At the dam site, Porter jumped on a horse and galloped to the vessels upstream. Only the *Lexington* had steam up. He ordered her to make a run for it. She pitched down the roaring torrent, hung for a moment on the rocks, and then swept through the gap and rounded to the bank in deep water, as the watching soldiers cheered wildly.

But eight of the big ironclads and a monitor were still left above the upper falls. The broken dam could only maintain the water level at a little over five feet, but the ships, even without guns and armor, drew over six. Bailey put his soldiers to work again. For three days, they labored in water up to their chests building two wing dams which would direct the water into the middle of the river, making a channel six and one-half feet deep. Then four of the ships, hatches battened down, raced through the channel like canoes shooting a rapid. They lost their rudders against jutting rocks, but were otherwise unharmed. Next day, the remaining ships followed them. The guns and ammunition, which had been sent overland to lighten the ships, were put back on board. The ironclads had left their armor behind, buried in Red River quicksand, but Northern mills soon made more.

The stubborn defenses and geographical obstacles of the South may have temporarily rebuffed the Union Navy, but the ironclads were still afloat and ready for the decisive battles that lay ahead.

8
"DAMN THE
TORPEDOES"

When Admiral Farragut arrived at the naval base in Pensacola, Florida, on January 17, 1864, everybody had "ram fever." It was persistently rumored that the Southerners had five ironclad rams in Mobile Bay, which were about to come out, break the blockade, destroy the Pensacola base, and recapture New Orleans. Farragut boarded a launch and went to see for himself. He got near enough to count the many guns in Fort Morgan at the entrance to the bay.

Farragut wrote to Secretary of the Navy Welles pleading for monitors to counter Southern guns and rams. Surely, he said, Admiral Porter could spare him some from the river fleet. He did not know that Porter was at that moment in grave danger of losing the inland ironclads up the Red River. Meanwhile, the North's saltwater ironclads were battering futilely at Charleston. It would be several months before Farragut received any armored vessels.

Fortunately for the North, however, Confederate Admiral Franklin Buchanan, who was in charge of the Mobile fleet, was in no position to break the blockade. The "ironclads" under his command were the *Tennessee, Tuscaloosa, Huntsville, Nashville,* and *Baltic.* But the last four were rams which did not have all their armor in place. Buchanan's most reliable ships were three unarmored gunboats and the mighty *Tennessee,* the strongest and largest of all the Confederate ironclads. She was armed with six rifled cannons, four in each broadside and two on pivots at the bow and stern. The ironclad was protected by a sloping casemate of wood two feet thick covered by six inches of iron at the ends and five inches on the sides. Her engines were less impressive. Salvaged from an old steamer, they were incapable of moving the heavy vessel any faster than six miles an hour. The weakest point of the *Tennessee* proved to be her steering chains, which for some unexplained reason, ran unprotected along the top of the deck from the casemate to the rudder.

For a time, however, it looked as though Buchanan might not be able to use the *Tennessee* at all.

The *Tennessee,* with a draft of fourteen feet, was stranded in the Alabama River, where the depth of the water over the bar stretching across the mouth of the river was only ten feet. The Confederates spent ten frantic weeks trying to free the ram. Finally, on May 18, immense pontoons attached to her hull lifted her high enough to be dragged over the bar into the bay.

During this time, Farragut had brought together an impressive Union fleet of fourteen wooden ships. He then learned that the new monitor *Manhattan* had left New York for the Gulf and would be followed soon by her sister ship, *Tecumseh.* He was advised, too, that two new double-turreted monitors, the *Winnebago* and the *Chickasaw,* were on their way down the Mississippi to join him. When the monitors all finally arrived, along with an army force to attack the harbor's defenses by land, Farragut decided to go into the bay. As always, he made careful plans. The wooden ships were to be lashed in pairs, a small vessel tied to each larger one on the side away from the main fort so that it could pull the bigger ship out of action if it became disabled. The pairs of ships were to steam through the channel in line of battle. The monitors would form a separate line slightly in advance of the wooden vessels and nearer to the fort. Farragut knew that the entrance to the bay was heavily mined, and that a buoy at the edge of the minefield marked the narrow channel between the field and the fort. He ordered all his captains to go up this channel.

The fleet got under way at 6:00 a.m. on August 5. The monitors, because of their slower speed, started first. By 6:30, the two leading monitors had opened a long-range duel with Fort Morgan. Soon after, the *Brooklyn*, the *Hartford* and the rest of the fleet joined the battle, their crews eager and excited after their long months of waiting.

The wooden ships were taking some punishment from the guns of Fort Morgan, but the attack was going according to plan. Then the leading monitor, *Tecumseh*, suddenly veered left and headed straight for the *Tennessee*, which had appeared behind the minefield. Watchers on the *Brooklyn* were stunned as the *Tecumseh*, in the next instant, careened sharply to one side and sank almost instantly. She had hit a mine. It happened so fast that ninety-three of the 114 men aboard went down with her.

One of the most heroic incidents of the battle was the rescue of ten survivors of the *Tecumseh* by a small boat manned by Acting Ensign Henry C. Nields, a boy in his teens, and six volunteers. The boat was launched amidst a hail of shells from Fort Morgan that splashed into the water around it. Ignoring the deadly fire, Nields and his crew rowed toward the men struggling in the water. Nields, who was steering, looked up and discovered that the flag was not flying from the staff above him. He took it from its case and raised it under the guns of the Confederate fort. This probably saved his life. A gunner on the *Hartford*, seeing a boat without a flag, had trained his hundred-pounder on it and was about to pull the lock string when the Stars and Stripes unfurled at the stern.

During the *Tecumseh*'s sinking, the *Brooklyn*, her engines stopped, was drifting out of the channel toward the minefield. Suddenly realizing her danger, she started to back up and threw the rest of the fleet into brief confusion. The flagship *Hartford* pulled alongside her. Admiral Farragut, in the shrouds where he had climbed to see over the smoke, signaled the *Brooklyn* to move ahead. When she hesitated, Farragut ordered the *Hartford* to pass her. Captain James Alden, Jr., of the *Brooklyn*, shouted a warning that there was a "heavy line of torpedoes across the channel." In answer, Farragut is alleged to have replied, "Damn the torpedoes. Full speed ahead!"

In any case, the fleet ignored the minefield and passed through it without further incident. Later it was discovered that most of the mines had leaked, making the wet powder harmless. Still, some remained lethal, and it was simply a matter of luck that no ship but the *Tecumseh* had been sunk.

As the *Hartford* forged ahead, three Confederate gunboats poured a merciless raking fire into her, an attack which the flagship answered with her bow and broadside guns. When the *Hartford* drew near the *Tennessee,* the Southern ironclad got under way and appeared to be heading for the flagship. But suddenly, the *Tennessee* swerved and headed for the other wooden ships hoping to find victims among them. Buchanan first tried to ram the *Brooklyn*, then the *Richmond,* and finally the *Lackawanna* - missing each in turn because of his ship's crawling speed. The best she could do was to fire a broadside into each ship as she passed, damaging the wooden ships only slightly. She received a broadside from each in return, which bounced harmlessly off her iron armor.

The *Tennessee* continued down the line of advancing vessels, firing into the *Monongahela,* the *Kennebec*, the *Ossipee,* and the *Oneida.* But when several monitors started firing at her, she retired under the guns of Fort Morgan, and there was a lull in the fighting.

The Union fleet anchored about four miles up the bay, and the men were called to breakfast. Farragut thought the fight was over, and that the *Tennessee* would remain under the guns of Fort Morgan. But Buchanan remembered what had happened to his first ironclad when it drew off and waited. After pacing back and forth on the gun deck while his men sought relief from the heat on the deck outside the casemate, Buchanan suddenly turned to the captain of the *Tennessee* and said, "Follow

them up, Johnston; we can't let them off that way."
So before the Union sailors had a chance to bite
into their hardtack, the ram was sighted coming up
the bay.

The *Tennessee* made directly for the *Hartford*, but
before reaching the flagship, she was struck by
the wooden ship *Monongahela*. The only effect
of the blow was to stave in the Union ship's bow
and break off her cutwater. Next, the *Lackawanna*
rammed the *Tennessee* with no better result. As the
ships separated, the *Lackawanna* came alongside
the ironclad. The two ships exchanged fire - the
gun crews of the *Lackawanna* trying to pick off
gunners through the *Tennessee's* ports. According
to one report, they also threw a spittoon and a
holystone at the Southerners, which did about as
much damage as their shells.

Now it was the *Hartford's* turn. As she rushed head
on at the *Tennessee*, the latter swerved. The sides
of the two ships grated together just as Farragut
climbed up the shrouds for a better view. The
Hartford started to come around for another attack,
but before she could, the *Lackawanna*, making her
second pass at the ram, missed and crashed into
the side of the Union flagship.

The admiral jumped down to inspect the damage
and found that the *Hartford*, luckily, had been
struck above the water line. He ordered her to
pursue the *Tennessee* along with the rest of the

fleet. With the ironclad *Manhattan* in the lead, and all guns ablaze, the Union ships slowly approached the Southern ironclad.

Lieutenant Wharton of the *Tennessee* described the *Manhattan's* attack: "A hideous looking monster came creeping up on our port side, whose slowly revolving turret revealed the cavernous depths of a mammoth gun. 'Stand clear of the port side!' I shouted. A moment after, a thundering report shook us all, while a blast of dense, sulphurous smoke covered our port holes, and 440 pounds of iron, propelled by sixty pounds of powder admitted daylight through our side." A subsequent hit by the *Manhattan* sent up a splatter of metal, one piece of which struck Buchanan's leg and broke it.

By this time, the monitor *Winnebago* had come up on the other side of the *Tennessee* and was pounding away at the Southern ironclad. The *Chickasaw* took a position off the stern and, at a range of ten yards, hammered at the end of the ship's casemate with the eleven-inch guns of her forward turret. It was this fire that finally defeated the *Tennessee*. An early shot destroyed part of her exposed rudder chains, leaving the ship unmaneuverable. Other hits knocked off her smokestack and jammed the shutters so that the stern gun could not be used. Finally, her iron plate began to fly off in chunks, leaving exposed the wood of the casemate.

Captain Johnston had succeeded to command when Buchanan was wounded. His survey of the ship disclosed that she could not be maneuvered to bring a gun to bear. Further fighting was hopeless and would lead only to the slaughter of the crew. Johnston climbed on deck and lowered the ship's ensign. "I then decided," he said later, "although with an almost bursting heart, to hoist the white flag, and returning onto the shield, placed it in the same spot where but a few moments before had floated the proud flag for whose honor I would so cheerfully have sacrificed my own life if I could possibly have become the only victim."

With the surrender of the gallant *Tennessee,* the Southern ironclads had fought their last battle; with the fall of Mobile the following April, the Confederacy retained but one major seaport - Wilmington, North Carolina. Here the Northern ironclads saw their last action. The *New Ironsides* and the monitors from Charleston broke down the defenses of Fort Fisher with an intense bombardment to prepare the way for an army landing that overwhelmed the fort. Two months later, all fighting ended with Robert E. Lee's surrender at Appomattox.

The world that watched four years of fraternal fighting in America learned many new things about warfare. Lee's use of trenches was new, as was the extensive use of mines. The repeating rifle was born and Dr. Richard Jordan Gatling's invention, called a machine gun, was introduced toward the end of the war. But the most dramatic military weapon to be tried in the Civil War was the ironclad. It had been an experiment when the fighting started; by the conclusion of the war, the obsolescence of the wooden warship had been conclusively demonstrated.

By 1865, ships with fixed broadside batteries were also considered by most progressive naval designers to be relics of the past. The heavily armored turret, which could be turned to fire at any number of different targets while the ship remained in one position, had, they believed, proved itself superior to all other naval designs.

Turrets were even planned for the North's costly monument to the broadside battery, the *Dunderberg* (thunder mountain). This last and largest of ironclads built for battle in the Civil War was 373 feet long from the tip of her massive ram to the blades of her twin, twenty-one-foot propellers. She was originally designed to carry two revolving casemates, but they were never built. Unfortunately for naval science, the Civil War ended before the *Dunderberg* could undergo her trial by cannon fire. Historians can only speculate on how her powerful guns might have hastened the Union victory.

After the war, the U.S. Navy kept improving on John Ericsson's original designs, building another generation of monitors that were not only packed with firepower but also seaworthy. One of these improved monitors, the *Miantonomoh*, easily crossed the Atlantic in spite of the four-foot waves washing over her low decks. Many of the new monitors were still in commission at the time of the United States war with Spain in 1898, and a few were even used for harbor defense as late as World War I.

Even today, the tough little ironclads of the Civil War live on in the huge warships of the world's modern navies - both armor plate and revolving turrets are features of nearly every fighting ship that sails the seas. The once revolutionary craft also survive in the spirit of experiment that still produces new ships for new emergencies, and in the spirit of adventure that impels men to serve at sea no matter what the hazards.